LEARNING
FROM
LINCOLN

ASCD MEMBER BOOK

Many ASCD members received this book as a
member benefit upon its initial release.

Learn more at: **www.ascd.org/memberbooks**

LEARNING
FROM
LINCOLN

Leadership Practices
for
School Success

HARVEY ALVY   PAM ROBBINS

Alexandria, Virginia USA

ASCD®

1703 N. Beauregard St. • Alexandria, VA 22311-1714 USA
Phone: 800-933-2723 or 703-578-9600 • Fax: 703-575-5400
Web site: www.ascd.org • E-mail: member@ascd.org
Author guidelines: www.ascd.org/write

Gene R. Carter, *Executive Director;* Judy Zimny, *Chief Program Development Officer;* Nancy Modrak, *Publisher;* Scott Willis, *Director, Book Acquisitions & Development;* Julie Houtz, *Director, Book Editing & Production;* Darcie Russell, *Senior Associate Editor;* Georgia Park, *Senior Graphic Designer;* Mike Kalyan, *Production Manager;* Marlene Hochberg, *Typesetter;* Kyle Steichen, *Production Specialist*

Printed in the United States of America. Cover art © 2010 by ASCD. Cover photo courtesy of Prints and Photographs Division, Library of Congress, LC-DIG-ppmsca-19195. Photo p. 177 courtesy of Prints and Photographs Division, Library of Congress, LC-USZ62-11897.

ASCD publications present a variety of viewpoints. The views expressed or implied in this book should not be interpreted as official positions of the Association.

All Web links in this book are correct as of the publication date below but may have become inactive or otherwise modified since that time. If you notice a deactivated or changed link, please e-mail books@ascd.org with the words "Link Update" in the subject line. In your message, please specify the Web link, the book title, and the page number on which the link appears.

ASCD Member Book, No. FY10-9 (Aug. 2010, P). ASCD Member Books mail to Premium (P), Select (S), and Institutional Plus (I+) members on this schedule: Jan., PSI+; Feb., P; Apr., PSI+; May, P; July, PSI+; Aug., P; Sept., PSI+; Nov., PSI+; Dec., P. Select membership was formerly known as Comprehensive membership.

PAPERBACK ISBN: 978-1-4166-1023-6   ASCD product #110036
Also available as an e-book (see Books in Print for the ISBNs).

Quantity discounts for the paperback edition only: 10–49 copies, 10%; 50+ copies, 15%; for 1,000 or more copies, call 800-933-2723, ext. 5634, or 703-575-5634. For desk copies: member@ascd.org.

Library of Congress Cataloging-in-Publication Data

Alvy, Harvey B.
  Learning from Lincoln : leadership practices for school success / Harvey Alvy and Pam Robbins.
     p. cm.
  Includes bibliographical references and index.
  ISBN 978-1-4166-1023-6 (pbk. : alk. paper)
  1. School management and organization. 2. Educational leadership. 3. Lincoln, Abraham, 1809-1865. I. Robbins, Pamela II. Title.
  LB2805.A464 2010
  371.2--dc22
                          2010014050

20 19 18 17 16 15 14 13 12 11 10   1 2 3 4 5 6 7 8 9 10 11 12

To Our Parents

Dan Alvy, a man of integrity,
and Cooper Union student 71 years after
Lincoln's "Right Makes Might" address

Rebecca Pearl Alvy, a champion
of all children

David J. Robbins, a lifelong leader
who believed that, in the end,
"it's all about relationships"

Muriel Robbins, a teacher,
counselor, and musician who continues
to inspire us with her wisdom, energy,
and personal example

LEARNING FROM LINCOLN

Leadership Practices for School Success

Acknowledgments

We are indebted to many professional educators and family members who by their example have helped to steer the direction of this book.

Pam Robbins would like to acknowledge Percy Haugen and Ernie Moretti, educators who provided inspiring induction experiences for her and created a strong sense of meaning and enthusiasm for her work. Special thanks are due to DD Dawson, Margaret Arbuckle, Terry Deal, Karen Dyer, Linda Gaidimas, Carl Glickman, Tony Gregorc, Roland Barth, Lynn Seay, Allen Haymon, Kent Peterson, Jane Scott, Dennis Sparks, Karen Steinbrink Koch, Leslie and Mike Rowland, Jeff White, Patrice Newnam, DeWitt House, David Mathis, Judy Mullins, Pat Montgomery, Helene Paroff, Kathleen McElroy, Lou Martin, Ann Cunningham-Morris, Debbie Brown, Debbie Howerton, Virginia Connelly, Gayle Gregory, Stephanie Hirsh, Tom Guskey, Jay McTighe, Betsy Dunnenberger, Judith Warren Little, Maurice Elias, Kelly Tonsmeire, Jean Smith, Tim Gaddis, Mike Bossi, Pat Wolfe, and the late Frank Gomez and Susan Loucks-Horsley for their professional colleagueship, insights, wisdom, thoughtful feedback, and willingness to collaborate. The late Jane Bailey deserves profound thanks for her energy, spirit, dedication, and unique ability to model the way professionally and personally. The late Judy Arin Krupp deserves special mention for her expertise regarding adult learning and for the inspiration she provided as a friend and professional colleague.

The courage and strength displayed by Stephanie Robbins Burlington, Pam's sister, as well as her commitment to children, have been a source of inspiration. Heartfelt thanks are due to Ray Cubbage for his sage advice, companionship, love, patience, support, and inspiration.

Harvey Alvy's first principal while teaching in the Harlem section of New York City, Lionel McMurren, will always serve as an example of an ethical leader who inspired new teachers to reach great heights. Harvey is especially indebted to the school leaders, teachers, school secretaries, university colleagues, students, and friends who have shared ideas, provided constructive criticism, and supported his journey as an elementary, middle, and high school teacher; elementary and secondary principal; and currently the William C. Shreeve Endowed Professor of Educational Administration at Eastern Washington University. These include Ted Coladarci, Jane Liu, Bob Gibson, Richard Shustrin, Alan Siegel, David Chojnacki, Steve Kapner, Forrest Broman, Elaine Levy, Leonie Brickman, Don Bergman, Roger and Betty Bicksler, Rob Beck, Joan Dickerson, Vince Aleccia, Kevin Pyatt, Alan Coelho, Mike Dunn, Carole Meyer, Abby Chill, Tammy Campbell, Larry Keller, Deb Clemens, Chris and Casey Tuckerman, Ken and Ellen Karcinell, Emeritus Professor of History Richard Donley, Nelson and Lisa File, Bob Connor, Konni deGoeij, Drew Alexander, Bob Stockton, Paul Schmidt, Jim and Sally Bogaert, Nicholas Russ, Sandy Bensky, Uma Maholtra, Les Portner, Billie Gehres, Sharon Jayne, Jim Howard, Steve Smedley, Ray Cubbage, Sharon Mowry, and the late Tom Overholt, Boni Rahaman, Phil Snowden, William C. Shreeve, and Len Foster. Harvey would also like to acknowledge the inspirational works written by Lincoln and Civil War historians Michael Burlington, David Herbert Donald, Doris Kearns Goodwin, John Hope Franklin, Harold Holzer, James McPherson, Douglas L. Wilson, and, in particular, Ronald C. White, whose book *A. Lincoln* (2009), and Spokane, Washington, lecture on Lincoln's Second Inaugural Address significantly influenced our endeavor.

To Norman Alvy and Vicki Alvy, "you're the best." Rebecca Eizabeth Alvy's love of life, humor, and passion for diversity and social justice exemplify the difference this generation is making. To Bonnie, your courage and love are sustaining.

Nancy Modrak, a visionary leader in her own right, deserves special recognition for her encouragement and support in the conceptual phase of this ASCD book. Scott Willis's guidance, enthusiasm, and suggestions during the first draft of the manuscript were invaluable. We are grateful to work with Darcie Russell once again. Kathleen Florio's ability to understand our intent as authors and communicate with precision has significantly enhanced the manuscript.

Finally, to our parents, as always, we are grateful.

Introduction

Abraham Lincoln. His life and work evoke possibility, humility, hope, and moral leadership. Frederick Douglass may have said it best. On April 14, 1876, Douglass was the keynote speaker at the dedication of the Freedmen's Monument in Washington, D.C. On this occasion, Douglass said of Lincoln:

> Though high in position, the humblest could approach him and feel at home in his presence. Though deep, he was transparent; though strong, he was gentle; though decided and pronounced in his convictions, he was tolerant toward those who differed from him, and patient under reproaches. . . . The hard condition of his early life, which would have depressed and broken down weaker men, only gave greater life, vigor, and buoyancy to the heroic spirit of Abraham Lincoln. (Oakes, 2007, pp. 270–271)

Lincoln's leadership helped a nation continue a journey toward equality—a journey that has not yet been completed.

As school leaders, we, too, are embarked upon an unfinished journey, a journey characterized by possibility and guided by the sacred proposition that "all men are created equal."* Lincoln's words and deeds related to equality and possibility serve as a beacon for all school leaders—principals, teachers, and superintendents—illuminating a keen focus on what is important in their work to help students realize the gift of democracy. Lincoln's beliefs

---

* To represent historical documents authentically, the term *men* appears in context; for the present day, we will, of course, be referring to men and women.

and actions also have profound implications for 21st century initiatives and challenges, such as closing the achievement gap and reducing the high school dropout rate. Lincoln knew that realizing possibility for every individual could not occur without the desire and opportunity to learn. His life story portrays that reality. Rising from humble roots, Lincoln achieved his goals through hard work, dedicated and focused independent study, and perseverance. In his classic biography of Lincoln, Benjamin Thomas (1952) notes:

> Education seemed to him the most important question a people could consider, for every man should have sufficient education to enable him to read the history of his own and of other countries, [then quoting Lincoln] "by which he may duly appreciate the value of our free institutions . . . to say nothing of the advantages and satisfaction derived from all being able to read the scriptures and other works, both of a religious and moral nature, for themselves." (p. 29)

Lincoln's words echo the beliefs of other well-known educational pioneers, such as Thomas Jefferson and Horace Mann, and female trailblazers, such as Catherine Beecher and Emma Hart Willard.

Story after story about Lincoln highlights his incredible ability to focus on the important work and put personality differences aside. Integrity was fundamental to Lincoln, and he adhered to values he held sacred, despite adversity or lack of popularity. He possessed strong beliefs about matters of principle. Although critics and allies complained that he was too cautious and slow to implement principles, Lincoln believed that his deliberate nature and political know-how strengthened his hand when he moved forward. He also regularly sought out opposing views in seeking to better understand an issue. He consistently demonstrated acts of caring with sincerity and healing words. He worked tirelessly on problems that deeply concerned him. He was able to look across the horizon of time and envision a desired future.

As citizens of Lincoln's tomorrow, we are, in a very real sense, renewed and inspired by his character, strength, and example. Lincoln represents the American dream. Moreover, his ideals captured the consciousness of the world. David Lloyd George, a former British prime minister, once said of

Lincoln, "He is one of those giant figures, of whom there are very few in history, who lose their nationality in death" (Carwardine, 2006, p. 323). It is a risk for our nation, and the world, to forget Lincoln's meaning.

Additionally, Lincoln's life offers another magnificent gift: his experiences serve as an entrée into the study of leadership practices and their consequences. Lincoln's life and leadership provide profound examples and lessons for school principals, teacher leaders, district leaders, and other individuals with leadership responsibilities.

This book is dedicated to the following question: What can educational leaders learn from an in-depth study of Lincoln's leadership experiences to achieve success in today's schools? The format invites the reader to study the Lincoln example, to examine stories of his leadership capacity, and then to reflect upon the meaning they convey and to generate 21st century applications. Thus this enduring example of past leadership will provide navigation tools for the arduous path to success in the future—by taking the reader on a journey anchored in cherished values and norms of collaboration and competence, and strengthened by an uplifting spirit of hope.

Lincoln's life serves as a context from which this book highlights 10 leadership qualities and skills that are important for school leaders. Through careful study of these vibrant leadership skills, demonstrated by Lincoln's example, the reader has an opportunity to examine theory through story and its timeless implications for day-to-day leadership practices and challenges. As readers analyze theory and practice, they can reflect also on Lincoln's successes and failures, wise decisions and missteps, to better understand the opportunities and challenges of today. Our vision as authors is that by studying Lincoln's example, his behaviors, and the 10 leadership qualities embodied in his beliefs and actions, school leaders will learn important lessons to clarify their own personal visions and to promote a shared vision that aligns their actions with the deeply cherished values of others, enlisting commitment and energy to a noble cause—the success of *each* student. This cause will serve as a compass to advance decision-making capabilities and to demonstrate daily acts of trust, rapport building, and respect that increase the competence and confidence of constituents and culminate in long-term success.

The 10 leadership qualities and skills we will discuss:

1. Implementing and sustaining a mission and vision with focused and profound clarity

2. Communicating ideas effectively with precise and straightforward language

3. Building a diverse and competent team to successfully address the mission

4. Engendering trust, loyalty, and respect through humility, humor, and personal example

5. Leading and serving with emotional intelligence and empathy

6. Exercising situational competence and responding appropriately to implement effective change

7. Rising beyond personal and professional trials through tenacity, persistence, resilience, and courage

8. Exercising purposeful visibility

9. Demonstrating personal growth and enhanced competence as a lifetime learner, willing to reflect on and expand ideas

10. Believing that hope can become a reality

Not surprisingly, the literature on school leadership practices linked to organizational success stresses many of the same qualities and skills (Cotton, 2003; DuFour & Eaker, 1998; *Educational Leadership Policy Standards*, ISLLC, 2008; Evans, 1996; Fullan, 2007; Glickman, Gordon, & Ross-Gordon, 2010; Marzano, Waters, & McNulty, 2005; Reeves, 2006; Robbins & Alvy, 2004; Sergiovanni, 2009) as those exemplified by Lincoln. Many of these critical qualities also are supported by research beyond the field of education (Bennis & Nanus, 1985; Collins, 2001, 2005; George, 2007; Goleman, Boyatzis, & McKee, 2002; Heifetz & Linsky, 2002; Kouzes & Posner, 2002; Zenger & Folkman, 2002). For example, stories abound regarding Lincoln's penchant for walking and talking with his military officers on and off the battlefield to develop situational awareness to guide future military and political actions and to gain a sense of empathy for the psychological and emotional states of those fighting the battle to achieve the desired future reality. Principals who spend time "in the trenches" can accomplish similar valuable outcomes. Both examples illustrate the critical link between leadership behaviors and organizational productivity resulting in superior staff (and student) performance.

To fully convey the power of these leadership qualities and skills, we devote a chapter to each of the 10 areas. We cite examples of the qualities and skills from Lincoln's life to illustrate the leadership concept being examined, and we use Lincoln's own words and actions, and the words of historians or his contemporaries, to support the leadership principle. As readers reflect on Lincoln's leadership skills, they should remember that the 10 areas of focus are interrelated. For example, without perseverance, the mission and vision of preserving the Union could not have been accomplished. Following each historical analysis of Lincoln's skills, we examine implications for 21st century leadership. Thus, the analysis of leadership based on Lincoln's life serves as a platform for school leaders to help them reflect upon the *past*, to refine and expand their *present* leadership practices, and to project the *future* implications for working with all the stakeholders in the school community.

It is important to note that the goal of this book is not to have readers attempt to replicate Lincoln's style and behavior. Leaders must find their own paths to success, exercising self-awareness and developing strengths, and working to improve weaknesses. They must learn from their own stories and discover why they have a passion for leadership. Each one of us, as leaders, must take a personal and distinctive journey if we are to succeed. We must be honest concerning what we learn from our journeys to lead authentically (George, 2007). However, we can find inspiration—and learn how to lead— by studying the courage and example of others.

A final critical point. This text tries to avoid venturing into the fog that sometimes obscures the reality of Lincoln's life—the successes and failures— with the myth of the perfect leader that began to emerge at the moment of his martyrdom. The reader should know, however, that the passion and inspiration for this work rest partially on questions that are unavoidable when examining Lincoln's life story—questions such as these: How could an individual from such humble beginnings, with a total experience of one year of formal schooling, rise to such heights? How did Lincoln remain resilient in the face of so many personal setbacks, including the death of his mother when he was 9, the loss of two children, bouts of depression throughout his life, and the incomprehensible tragedy of the Civil War? Lincoln was seemingly able to labor on individually, and he carried a nation with him. This ability to grow and persevere despite adversity is a compelling characteristic and worthy of study. Finally, Lincoln's life is inspirational because it represents hope. Lincoln believed in people and in the possibility that great accomplishments could be realized if people believed in the power of ideas and the power of individuals to become better persons (Ferguson, 2007; Phillips, 1992).

It is with this backdrop that we venture into the past to understand our present reality and to illuminate our future.

CHAPTER ONE

Implementing and Sustaining
a Mission and Vision with Focused
and Profound Clarity

> By *itself*, preservation of the Union was an empty concept to Lincoln, unless the Union remained dedicated—or could forcibly be rededicated—to its founding principle that all men are created equal.
>
> —Richard Striner, *Father Abraham: Lincoln's Relentless Struggle to End Slavery*, p. 7 (emphasis in original)

Defining leadership, especially great leadership, is a difficult task. In their classic book *Leaders*, Bennis and Nanus (1985) state:

> Multiple interpretations of leadership exist, each providing a sliver of insight but each remaining an incomplete and wholly inadequate explanation. . . . It's as if what Braque once said about art is also true of leadership, "The only thing that matters in art is the part that cannot be explained." (pp. 4–5)

Yet, despite the difficulty of coming to a consensus on how we can measure successful leadership, there is almost universal agreement that *success in carrying out the mission and vision of an endeavor—a cause—should be a primary gauge of leadership success*. Jim Collins (2005) in *Good to Great and the Social Sectors* hails the qualities of what he describes as "Level 5 leaders." These leaders are "ambitious first and foremost for the cause, the movement, the mission, the work—*not themselves*—and they have the will to do (whatever it takes) to make good on that ambition" (p. 11, emphasis in original). In another context, Collins states that these leaders display "a paradoxical blend of personal humility and professional will" (p. 12). Not surprisingly, Collins (2005, May) cites Lincoln as a Level 5 leader who "never wavered" despite the devastating casualties at the "victorious" Battle of Antietam in 1862 and who resolved to continue the war to preserve the original mission of the Union and the evolving mission toward emancipation.

In fact, Lincoln used the limited victory at Antietam as the opportunity to publicly announce that the Emancipation Proclamation would be issued on January 1, 1863. His judgment in using Antietam as the opportune time to introduce the proclamation is an example of Lincoln's genius for seizing the moment and gauging what the majority of the Northern population, although reluctant in some quarters, was ready to accept. Opportune timing is, of course, a critical skill for all leaders.

When analyzing Lincoln's focus and clarity concerning mission and vision during the Civil War years, it is helpful to consider his thinking on a macro level (large scale) related to national interests and on a micro level (local scale) related to individual opportunity. For example, on a macro level Lincoln was in charge of several critical wartime responsibilities: "He performed or oversaw five wartime functions . . . in diminishing order of personal involvement: policy, national strategy, military strategy, operations, and tactics" (McPherson, 2008a, p. 5). Other macro responsibilities related to keeping the Northern states' and—maybe more strategically important—the border states' morale and national will focused on victory based on a just cause. Thus, communication with newspapers, politicians, the Congress, and foreign countries needed to be managed successfully to maintain the resolve to win.

On the micro or local level, Lincoln believed that the war would decide whether individual opportunity as part of the democratic experiment would succeed. Thus he often viewed the events of the war on a personal level emanating from his own worldview and experiences concerning possibility: a democratic nation will reward individual merit and transform lives. Lincoln sought opportunities to engage in conversation every day with soldiers or citizens to press the national interest, the importance of the war, and reasons to continue the fight. For example, he said the following to a regiment of Ohio soldiers returning home from battle on August 22, 1864:

> I almost always feel inclined, when I happen to say anything to soldiers, to impress upon them in a few brief remarks the importance of success in this contest. It is not merely for today, but for all time to come that we should perpetuate for our children's children this great and free government, which we have enjoyed all of our lives. I beg you to remember this, not merely for my sake, but for yours. I happen temporarily to occupy this big White House. I am a living witness that any one of your children may look to come here as my father's child has. (Basler, 1953–1955, Vol. VII, p. 512)

Mission and Vision Concerning the National Interest

In the United States, the chief executive serves as both the president of a nation and the military commander in chief. Presidents constantly face the realization that military strategy must align with national goals. Otherwise, during wartime, achieving military objectives may not be worthy of the struggle and ultimate sacrifice that war necessitates. Thus, a mission should not have loose ends—a military victory must lead to and support a nation's overarching mission. To illustrate, consider the final paragraph of Lincoln's annual message to Congress on December 1, 1862:

> Fellow-citizens, we cannot escape history. We of this Congress and this administration will be remembered in spite of ourselves. No personal significance, or insignificance, can spare one or another of us. The fiery trial through which we pass, will light us down, in honor or dishonor, to the latest generation. We say we are for the Union. The world will not forget that we say this. We know how to save the Union. The world knows we do know how to save it. We—even we here—hold the power, and bear the responsibility. In giving freedom to the slave, we assure freedom to the free—honorable alike in what we give, and what we preserve. We shall nobly save, or meanly lose, the last best hope of earth. Other means may succeed; this could not fail. The way is plain, peaceful, generous, just—a way which, if followed, the world will forever applaud, and God must forever bless. (Basler, 1953–1955, Vol. V, p. 537)

What is most striking about this document is the far-reaching consequences that Lincoln believed the war would have—not only for the United States, but for the world. Today, words such as "the last best hope of earth" may sound jingoistic, but in the 1860s American democracy was still a relatively new experiment, less than 100 years old. Lincoln saw democracy as a fragile experiment, and one in which success was not yet assured. The Civil War would determine the fate of democracy; Lincoln knew this.

The year 1862 was only a few generations removed from the revolutionary period in which a democracy had emerged, carved out of a British colony ruled by a European monarch. Heroes of the revolution were still alive when Lincoln was a youth.

The 1862 annual message also reveals Lincoln's development concerning the issue of slavery. Before the war, he was firm about holding to his interpretation of the Constitution—permitting slavery in defined states and territories but refusing to compromise on the expansion of slavery. And, although he considered various solutions concerning the abolition of slavery (including the very controversial option of supporting the foreign colonization of former slaves), the 1862 message provides insight into his development on the slavery question and the postwar possibilities of ex-slaves. These possibilities led, eventually, not only to emancipation, but also to Lincoln's public suggestion on the White House balcony on the evening of April 11, 1865, that some qualified former slaves in Louisiana should have voting rights. Voting rights for former slaves was a radical notion at the time. Not coincidentally, John Wilkes Booth swore to carry out his deadly conspiracy upon hearing Lincoln's words at the White House on that same evening. Booth acted three days later.

The "last best hope" idea also provides insight into Lincoln's vision of how each group suffers when one group is maligned. This was not a new idea for Lincoln. In 1855, when discussing the hatred of the Know-Nothing Party for immigrants and blacks, Lincoln wrote to his best friend, Joshua Speed:

> I am not a Know-Nothing. That is certain. How could I be? How can any one who abhors the oppression of negroes, be in favor of degrading classes of white people? Our progress in degeneracy appears to me to be pretty rapid. As a nation, we began by declaring that "all men are created equal." We now practically read it "all men are created equal, except

negroes." When the Know-Nothings get control, it will read "all men are created equal, except negroes, and foreigners, and Catholics." (Basler, 1953–1955, Vol. II, p. 323)

A compelling mission and vision should have personal meaning to all those who may be affected by the idea. Clearly, that was the case with Lincoln.

As commander in chief, Lincoln knew that to accomplish the mission, his war aims could not succeed simply by keeping Confederate troops off Northern soil. In fact, he never referred to, or verbally talked about, two separate nations or a separate "Confederate States of America." He did not refer to a "North" and "South" of Union and Confederate troops. Lincoln maintained that certain states were in rebellion against the Union; they were *not* the Confederate States of America. Also, he was firm about the military mission. When Union general Meade told Lincoln that his troops had succeeded in keeping Lee off Northern territory at Gettysburg in July 1863, a frustrated and angry Lincoln stated, "The whole country is our soil" (Donald, 1995, p. 446). And when Union general Hooker suggested taking Richmond after the Battle of Chancellorsville, Lincoln firmly noted that "Lee's Army, and not Richmond, is your true objective point" (Donald, 1995, p. 439). As Winik (2001) states, "No man was more fervent in his belief in the Union, no man loved his country, North as well as South, as much as Lincoln. And no man was more concerned about not simply winning the war, but about keeping the country and the nation together" (p. 242).

Later generations recognized the unique mission and challenge that Lincoln faced as much more than saving a union; maybe later generations could see Lincoln's vision better than those who witnessed the events of the Civil War years. For example, one of the most profound and clearly articulated explanations of Lincoln's mission occurred during the dedication of the Lincoln Memorial in 1922. Andrew Ferguson (2007) points out that in Germany, Bismarck helped to consolidate and create a union, as did Garibaldi in Italy; but in Lincoln's case it was a *particular kind of union* that was being fostered. Ferguson notes that at the dedication ceremony on May 30, 1922, the president of Tuskegee Institute, Robert Moton, the son of slaves, eloquently described the Lincoln achievement:

> The claim of greatness for Abraham Lincoln lies in this, that amid doubt
> and distrust, against the counsel of his chosen advisors, in the hour
> of the nation's utter peril, he put his trust in God and spoke the word
> that gave freedom to a race, and vindicated the honor of a nation con-
> ceived in liberty and dedicated to the proposition that all men are cre-
> ated equal. (p. 266)

Thus we see that Lincoln's purpose was realized because he understood the mission and vision and wavered from neither. The mission of union and equality could be realized only if a vision emerged of a nation that not only treated people equally but also could implement the democratic principles necessary to extend freedom and possibility to all.

Maybe the best historical example of a mission statement, with a rationale and an aligned vision clearly noted, is the Gettysburg Address (see Figure 1.1), which Lincoln delivered at the dedication ceremony for a national soldiers cemetery at Gettysburg. For the thousands who witnessed the address on November 19, 1863, and the millions who have studied the address since, the brief 272-word document leaves no doubt of the mission—equality and union; and the vision—a new birth of freedom and a government of the people, by the people, for the people. Edward Everett, the most renowned orator in the United States at the time and the primary speaker during the Gettysburg dedication, was one of the few to immediately realize the significance of Lincoln's remarks. Three days after the event he wrote to Lincoln, "I should be glad, if I could flatter myself that I came as near the central idea of the occasion in two hours, as you did in two minutes" (White, 2009, p. 609).

In addition to articulating a concise mission and vision, the Gettysburg Address points to other leadership qualities that characterize Lincoln. For example, the humility of successful leaders is often a most admired trait, a trait that helps build collaboration and respect among colleagues. Is there a more humble phrase in the English language than Lincoln's statement "The world will little note, nor long remember what we say here"? Hence, the greatness of the Gettysburg Address, to some extent, is a result of the humility that Lincoln felt in honoring "the brave men, living and dead" who sacrificed for the nation. We return to the Gettysburg Address in later chapters.

Figure 1.1
The Gettysburg Address

Four score and seven years ago our fathers brought forth on this continent, a new nation, conceived in Liberty, and dedicated to the proposition that all men are created equal.

Now we are engaged in a great civil war, testing whether that nation, or any nation so conceived and so dedicated, can long endure. We are met on a great battle-field of that war. We have come to dedicate a portion of that field, as a final resting place for those who here gave their lives that that nation might live. It is altogether fitting and proper that we should do this.

But, in a larger sense, we can not dedicate—we can not consecrate— we can not hallow—this ground. The brave men, living and dead, who struggled here, have consecrated it, far above our poor power to add or detract. The world will little note, nor long remember what we say here, but it can never forget what they did here. It is for us the living, rather, to be dedicated here to the unfinished work which they who fought here have thus far so nobly advanced. It is rather for us to be here dedicated to the great task remaining before us—that from these honored dead we take increased devotion to that cause for which they gave the last full measure of devotion—that we here highly resolve that these dead shall not have died in vain—that this nation, under God, shall have a new birth of freedom—and that government of the people, by the people, for the people, shall not perish from the earth.

—Abraham Lincoln

Lincoln's Life and Work: Implications for School Leaders

Successful school leaders possess a strong sense of responsibility and a deep and unwavering commitment to developing and carrying out a shared mission and vision, aligned with deeply held values and beliefs that focus on equity, social justice, democracy, and creating those conditions under which profound levels of human learning can flourish. Though much has transpired in our world since Lincoln's time, he nonetheless continues to "model the way" for leaders in general (Kouzes & Posner, 2002, p. 14). We glean from his work and his life precious attributes, such as focus and humility, that we aspire to emulate. And from his endeavors and accomplishments we find guidance for our own work as school leaders. From his struggles we derive lessons about adhering to deeply held beliefs, practicing ethical leadership, putting the cause first and personalities aside, and steadfastly pursuing leadership work dedicated to the conviction that all individuals are created equal, deserving of and desiring a genuine opportunity to leave their mark on the world.

If carrying out the mission and vision of an endeavor—a cause—is a primary gauge of successful leadership (Collins, 2005), then a starting point for the school leader's journey is self-knowledge. Leaders must know the causes they think and feel most passionately about. Bill George (2007) reminds us, "First, you have to understand yourself, because the hardest person you will ever have to lead is yourself" (p. xxxviii). Lincoln may have reflected deeply on issues before taking a firm stand, but once his mind was made up, he remained steadfast in carrying out the mission. Lincoln understood himself, and in the face of adversity he did not waver from his core values and beliefs. This does not mean that he saw little value in opposing viewpoints. If anything, these views helped further clarify his own. For example, late one evening in the White House, while preparing remarks, Lincoln sought an audience to listen to a draft of his writing. William O. Stoddard, a personal secretary, recalled that Lincoln said to him:

> "Sit down, I can always tell more about a thing after I've heard it read aloud, and know how it sounds. Just the reading of it to myself doesn't answer as well, either." . . . Stoddard then stated, "I don't know, Mr.

President, that I'd care to criticize anything you'd written." The President replied, "Yes, you will. Everybody else will. It's just what I want you to do. Sit still now, and you'll make as much of an audience as I call for." (Wilson, 2006, pp. 182–183)

Leaders can derive from this poignant example a core leadership competency related to self-knowledge: before developing a meaningful *shared* vision and mission, it is essential to first understand, articulate, and write out a *personal* vision. Doing so helps to clarify and galvanize thoughts and feelings. Through these actions a leader discovers the following:

• What drives me and ignites my passion and commitment to pursue a shared vision?

• What are those core values that underlie my fierce resolve to do whatever it takes to advance the organization's purpose and to ensure that every individual within the organization thrives?

Knowing what motivates oneself is a critical first step in the journey to create and realize a shared vision and mission. The shared vision and mission articulate, with profound clarity, organizational members' treasured values and their understanding of a desired future state, and serve to motivate every member of the organization to act in order to make that future state a reality. The earlier example of Lincoln speaking to a regiment of Ohio soldiers illustrates how the act of pursuing a shared vision and mission transcends the present and influences future reality. Leaders might, upon reading Lincoln's words to the soldiers, reflect by asking the following questions:

• What do I want to perpetuate in our schools, not merely for today but for all time to come?

• Though, as leader, my "temporary residence" may be the schoolhouse or the central office, what do I want future leaders who occupy the space to do or say to continue the work that I have begun?

• What do we want any one of our children or children's children to experience here?

Reflecting on History and the Moment: Implications for the Future

Lincoln's life, work, and words communicated the notion that a compelling mission and vision should have personal meaning for all those who may have been affected by the ideas embodied in his historical words. Further, Lincoln's purpose was realized because he understood the mission and vision and wavered from neither, seizing the historical opportunities to achieve his goals. His personal attributes—especially humility—helped build the collaboration, trust, and respect critical to accomplishing his purpose.

Interestingly, the current and much respected literature and research on leadership behaviors and their relationship to school and student success often mirror the attributes of Lincoln's example (Cotton, 2003; Marzano et al., 2005). Thinking about the implications for the future, consider the leadership work in which you are currently engaged and ask yourself the following questions:

- Are the goals such that they will transcend time?

- Who are the other significant players, critical to the accomplishment of the goals embodied in the vision or mission? What is their level of commitment and expertise?

- What personal leadership attributes do I possess that will help galvanize collective action toward the accomplishment of the vision?

- How will the vision and mission make the life and future of every child better and more promising?

- What thoughts inspired by Lincoln's legacy will influence my life's leadership work and practice?

Being able to accomplish great things as leaders requires specific character traits, qualities, and skills. Among the traits often mentioned as typifying Lincoln are empathy, humility, the ability to communicate, the capacity for growth, perspective taking, and a sense of humor. As a leader you may wish to reflect on your own character traits, leadership qualities and skills, strengths (and weaknesses) that will fuel (or diminish) your capacity to serve. You can use the following form to record your thoughts and perceptions.

Leadership Attributes and My School's Mission and Vision		
Leadership Qualities, Traits, and Skills Critical to My School Leadership Role	How These Qualities, Traits, and Skills Connect to Accomplishing the Mission and Vision	Self-Assessment: My Strengths and Weaknesses
1.		
2.		
3.		
4.		
5.		

Use the following space to jot down any other ideas, insights, or new perspectives from this chapter that you wish to add to your repertoire as a school leader.

CHAPTER TWO

Communicating Ideas Effectively with Precise and Straightforward Language

I have made this letter longer than usual, because I lacked the time to make it short.

—Blaise Pascal

Effective leaders are able to articulate their most important ideas with clarity, and they use language that emotionally connects with their audience. Connection creates meaning, and change will not occur unless a message is meaningful to an individual. Writing about successful school change, Evans (1996) stresses that successful leadership "practice is marked by a primary bias toward *clarity and focus*" (p. 206, emphasis in original). This chapter emphasizes Lincoln's ability to use everyday language with exquisite precision to inspire and articulate the national mission and vision to each segment of society.

Lincoln did not become an effective communicator easily. He experimented with language and intentional communication strategies throughout his life to improve his speaking and writing abilities. For example, Lincoln's longtime Springfield law partner, William Herndon, recalled that Lincoln would often sit at his desk reading aloud, listening to how words sounded before he gave a speech (Herndon, 1889/1970). Garry Wills (1992), in his Pulitzer Prize–winning book, *Lincoln at Gettysburg: The Words That Remade America*, states, "This, surely, is the secret of Lincoln's eloquence. He not only read aloud, to think his way into sounds, but wrote as a way of ordering his thoughts" (p. 162). Historians William Miller (2002) and Douglas Wilson (2006) describe the hard work and critical elements that resulted in Lincoln's extraordinary writing skills. Miller states, "As it is said that writers of great prose often start as writers of bad poetry . . . so it may be said that this writer [Lincoln] of great short speeches started by writing bad long ones" (p. 146). In *Lincoln's Sword*, a book dedicated to analyzing Lincoln's speeches and writings, Wilson notes, "What is most astonishing about Lincoln's performance in this regard is that he managed to bring his language within the range of ordinary vocabularies without cheapening his expression and, if anything, lending it even greater dignity" (p. 281).

The Power of Practice

Again, we must ask, how did Lincoln hone his communication skills with so little formal education? Two points seem to emerge from the historical record. First, his curiosity and determination to understand ideas and communicate their meaning were a powerful force from an early age. Second, he used a common but often overlooked strategy that is linked to the very talented: he practiced. During the winter of 1860, while in New England, Lincoln alluded to both points when he told the Reverend John Gulliver the following:

> I remember how, when a mere child, I used to get irritated when anybody talked to me in a way I could not understand. . . . I could not sleep, though I often tried to, when I got on such a hunt after an idea, until I caught it; and when I thought I had got it, I was not satisfied until I had repeated it over and over, till I had put it in language plain enough, as I thought, for any boy I knew to comprehend. This was a kind of passion with me. (Holzer, 2004, p. 200)

Zenger and Folkman (2002) highlight the importance of desire and practice in their research on extraordinary leaders. They note the common misconception that prodigies or the very talented just depend on their innate skills. Nothing is further from the truth. The most successful experts in music or other fields practice approximately 10,000 hours over a 10-year period. "One implication of this research is that some great leaders are not born with, but acquire at an early age, the desire to make things happen with other people. . . . Bad leaders assume that deliberate practice makes no difference, so they continue to perform but never improve" (pp. 44–45). From everything we know about Lincoln, the desire to improve was a lifelong characteristic.

Skills of an Effective Communicator

When examining Lincoln's extraordinary ability to communicate with eloquence, certain skills stand out: crisp, concise writing; an ability to use everyday language understood by the most and least educated; a desire to receive feedback and refine his works; mastering the primary communication media of his age—the telegraph and the newspaper; and the patience to listen to all sides to make effective decisions.

Crisp and Concise Writing

Lincoln learned that providing a brief explanation of an important issue orally or in writing was a difficult task. But he knew it was necessary. He stated, "Lawyers are not known for their brevity, and lawyers' briefs are rarely brief" (Ayres, 1992, p. 33). Ayres notes Lincoln's criticism of a particularly verbose lawyer: "It's like the lazy preacher who used to write long sermons, and the explanation was, he got to writin' and was too lazy to stop" (p. 33). Addressing the same issue, President Woodrow Wilson said, "If I am to speak for ten minutes, I need a week for preparation; if fifteen minutes, three days, if half an hour, two days, if an hour, I am ready now" (Wilson, 2006, p. 229).

Lincoln's ability to make a concise and precise point was demonstrated near the end of the seventh and final debate with Senator Stephen Douglas at Alton, Illinois, on October 15, 1858. Lincoln and Douglas were competing for one of the Illinois seats in the U.S. Senate. In response to Douglas's comments on slavery, Lincoln concisely stated:

> They are the two principles that have stood face to face from the beginning of time; and will ever continue to struggle. The one is the common right of humanity and the other the divine right of kings. It is the same principle in whatever shape it develops itself. It is the same spirit that

says: You work and toil and earn bread, and I'll eat it. (Basler, 1953–
1955, Vol. III, p. 315)

History reminds us that although Senator Douglas was reelected to the Senate by the state legislature in 1858, it was Lincoln's performance during the
debates that catapulted him to a national stage.

Everyday Language

Lincoln's communication appealed to a wide audience because his words
conveyed a clear message based on concrete ideas, delivered with metaphors,
stories, and figurative language. He wanted the audience to know exactly what
he meant. As a self-taught learner, he was familiar with leading books of the
day, including the King James Bible, Aesop's fables, and the plays of Shakespeare; he also enjoyed Lord Byron and Robert Burns. However, his greatest
asset in appealing to a wide audience was likely his modest, rural, agricultural
background. In a fascinating essay, "How Lincoln Won the War with Metaphor," James M. McPherson (1991) astutely notes the following:

> Instead of spending years inside the four walls of a classroom, Lincoln
> worked on frontier dirt farms most of his youth, he split rails, he rafted
> down the Mississippi on a flatboat, he surveyed land, he worked in a
> store where he learned to communicate with farmers and other residents
> of a rural community. Lincoln grew up close to the rhythms of nature,
> of wild beasts and farm animals, of forest and running water, of seasons
> and crops and of people who got their meager living from the land.
> These things, more than books, furnished his earlier education. They
> infused his speech with the images of nature. (pp. 94–95)

Consider how Lincoln used metaphor in the following four examples cited by
McPherson (1991):

During his 1860 New York speech at Cooper Union, Lincoln addressed
the southern secession threat to leave the Union if a Republican was elected
president:

> But you will not abide the election of a Republican President! In that
> supposed event, you say, you will destroy the union; and then, you say,

the great crime of having destroyed it will be upon us! That is cool. A highwayman holds a pistol to my ear, and mutters through his teeth, "Stand and deliver, or I shall kill you, and then you will be a murderer." (Basler, 1953–1955, Vol. III, pp. 546–547)

Lincoln's opposition to the spread of slavery as a moral wrong is clearly addressed in this speech he gave in New England in 1860, again with colorful metaphors:

> If I saw a venomous snake [i.e., slavery] crawling in the road, any man would say I might seize the nearest stick and kill it; but if I found that snake in bed with my children, that would be another question. I might hurt the children more than the snake, and it might bite them. . . . But if there was a bed newly made up, to which the children were to be taken, and it was proposed to take a batch of young snakes and put them there with them, I take it no man would say there was any question how I ought to decide. . . . That is just the case! The new Territories are the newly made bed to which our children are to go, and it lies with the nation to say whether they shall have snakes mixed up with them or not. It does not seem as if there could be much hesitation what our policy should be! (Basler, 1953–1955, Vol. IV, p. 18)

On June 16, 1858, Lincoln was nominated in Chicago as the Republican Senate candidate. His most famous antebellum metaphor, echoing biblical references, emerged during his acceptance speech when referring to the North-South conflict:

> A house divided against itself cannot stand. I believe this government cannot endure, permanently half *slave* and half *free*. I do not expect the union to be *dissolved*—I do not expect the house to *fall*—but I *do* expect it will cease to be divided. It will become *all* one thing, or *all* another. (Basler, 1953–1955, Vol. II, p. 461, emphasis in original)

In August 1863, Lincoln was asked to attend a public rally in Illinois supporting the war. Although he was unable to attend, he wrote a letter to his friend James Conkling, to be read at the rally. The Emancipation Proclamation, the inclusion of black soldiers in the fighting, and recent Northern battlefield victories, including Vicksburg on the Mississippi and Gettysburg in Pennsylvania, served as the backdrop for Lincoln's remarks. Lincoln knew that the letter would also be published in newspapers across the nation. Leaders are expected to succinctly communicate the mission—and at times inspire. Lincoln's remarks did both:

> The signs look better. The Father of Waters again goes unvexed to the sea. . . . And while those who have cleared the great river may well be proud, even that is not all. It is hard to say that anything has been more bravely, and well done, than at Antietam, Murfreesboro, Gettysburg, and on many fields of lesser note. . . . Peace does not appear so distant as it did. . . . It will then have been proved that, among free men, there can be no successful appeal from the ballot to the bullet; and that they who take such appeal are sure to lose their case, and pay the cost. And then, there will be some black men who can remember that, with silent tongue, and clenched teeth, and steady eye, and well-poised bayonet, they have helped mankind on to this great consummation; while, I fear, there will be some white ones, unable to forget that, with malignant heart, and deceitful speech, they have strove to hinder it. (Basler, 1953–1955, Vol. VI, pp. 409–410)

Seeking and Using Feedback

Individual or collective feedback is vital for individual or organizational success. Zenger and Folkman (2002) suggest that feedback is essential if good leaders are to become great. Lincoln thrived on feedback and, as mentioned earlier, practice. While preparing his First Inaugural Address in 1861, Lincoln sought feedback from many sources, including friends and politicians in Illinois, but primarily from his nominated secretary of state, William Seward. Although Lincoln did not use all of Seward's feedback, the secretary's suggestion to temper the address to make it more palatable to the South clearly impressed the president-elect. As a result, the address, delivered on March 4, 1861, conveyed the conciliatory tone suggested by Seward. The closing of the address includes some of the most famous words of any American president:

> In *your* hands, my dissatisfied fellow countrymen, and not in *mine*, is the momentous issue of civil war. . . . I am loath to close. We are not

enemies, but friends. We must not be enemies. Though passion may have strained, it must not break our bonds of affection. The mystic chords of memory, stretching from every battle-field, and patriot grave, to every living heart and hearthstone, all over this broad land, will yet swell the chorus of the Union, when again touched, as surely they will be, by the better angels of our nature. (Basler, 1953–1955, Vol. IV, p. 271, emphasis in original)

Mastering the Media—Telegraph and Newspapers

Leaders in today's world are constantly trying to adapt and learn how to use various media to communicate effectively. Often we assume that our challenge is greater than in the past. But since the Industrial Revolution, each generation of leaders has faced the question: What is the most effective means of communicating with the public? Lincoln faced this communication challenge. For example, using the telegraph effectively as a military resource was still a relatively new strategy during the Civil War. Yet Lincoln often used the War Department telegraph office next door to the office of Secretary of War Edwin M. Stanton on a daily basis—day and night. He would read hundreds of military dispatches and send out replies to his officers, at times personally directing military strategy (Cohen, 2002). As the war progressed, this tool became indispensible.

In addition, the importance of newspapers in Lincoln's time cannot be overstated. To win the war it was paramount for Lincoln to keep the Northern and border state constituencies on his side. At times support for the Union cause was certainly touch and go—and from many citizens, even in the North, Lincoln *never* fully gained the needed support. But he understood the importance of trying. According to White (2009),

> In 1862, he worked hard to listen to the public to find more ways to communicate his vision for the Union. He found the answer in newsprint. . . . At the time of Lincoln's birth, there were approximately 250 American newspapers. By the beginning of the Civil War, there were more than 2,500 newspapers, both daily and weekly. . . . Lincoln was a newspaper junkie. . . . Instead of writing letters to the editor, editors wrote letters to Lincoln. . . . And Lincoln also wrote letters. (p. 501)

Probably the most famous letter that Lincoln wrote during the war was a response to Horace Greeley, editor of the *New York Tribune*, penned on August 22, 1862. Lincoln was responding to Greeley's criticism that he was moving too slowly on emancipation. August 1862 was a dark period of the war for Lincoln. The South was holding its own, and many in the Northern and border states were resisting Lincoln's policies. Lincoln's calculated words to Greeley to hold the Union together are still debated today:

> My paramount objective in this struggle *is* to save the Union, and is *not* either to save or destroy slavery. If I could save the Union without freeing *any* slave I would do it, and if I could save it by freeing *all* the slaves I would do it; and if I could save it by freeing some and leaving others alone I would also do that. What I do about slavery, and the colored race, I do because I believe it helps to save the Union. . . . I have here stated my purpose according to my view of *official* duty; and I intend no modification of my oft-expressed *personal* wish that all men every where could be free. (Basler, 1953–1955, Vol. V, pp. 388–389, emphasis in original)

The intent of the letter was clear: to preserve the Union, Lincoln needed to hold his Northern and border state supporters—although those who believed in immediate emancipation would be greatly disappointed by his remarks. Interestingly, when the Greeley letter is used in history textbooks, the section parsing Lincoln's official and personal views is often omitted. Also, it is important to note that Lincoln had already presented a draft of the Emancipation Proclamation to his cabinet on July 22, 1862—yet for political reasons he decided not to tip his hand at that moment to Greeley, although the editor would certainly have welcomed hearing about the document.

The Patient Listener

Lincoln's skills as a successful Illinois lawyer were well known to those who worked with him on the judicial circuit during the 1840s and '50s. He was successful, in part, because while in court he would patiently listen to the other side, often conceding minor points as he developed his own strategy. A characteristic that sometimes unnerved other lawyers, friends, and politicians was his patient capacity to listen and weigh issues from all sides, while concealing his viewpoint.

This skill—patient listening—served Lincoln and the nation well during his presidency. Manisha Sinha (2008), in her essay "Allies for Emancipation? Lincoln and Black Abolitionists," argues that Lincoln's listening skills enabled him to evolve on the issue of emancipation and slowly but eventually come to the side of the abolitionists. "Lincoln's famous ability to listen to all sides of the story may not have served abolitionists well when it came to border state slaveholders and northern conservatives, but it did bode well for their own role as the staunchest supporters of emancipation" (p. 169). Sinha suggests that the unprecedented access that abolitionists and African Americans had to the president during his administration significantly influenced Lincoln's thinking.

Authentic two-way communication can only lead to sincere dialogue if each side is respected. For Lincoln, communication was more than a tool used to express his position on preserving the Union; it contributed to his enduring legacy because he eventually listened to and embraced the views of those who opposed not only the expansion of slavery but also the existence of slavery anywhere in the United States. These views led to a policy change that demanded the elimination of slavery as an American institution and the adoption of the Thirteenth Amendment to the Constitution.

Lincoln's Life and Work: Implications for School Leaders

In this chapter, we have addressed five aspects of communication associated with the leadership of President Lincoln: crisp and concise writing; using everyday language, including metaphors, understood by everyone; requesting and receiving feedback to refine one's work; mastering the media of telegraph and newspapers (contemporary media); and patient listening. Today's successful school leaders—principals, assistant principals, teacher leaders, central office staff, and superintendents—know that precision in communication is critical to their work (and tenure!). Their realization may have been a consequence of successful interactions or of errors in communication that served as learning experiences.

Marzano and colleagues (2005), citing various research studies, note that "communication might be considered the glue that holds together all the other responsibilities of leadership" (pp. 46–47). Responsibilities of leaders include facilitating teacher interaction and accessibility to teachers, and keeping lines of communication open with staff, students, community, and central office personnel. Marzano et al. suggest several specific communication responsibilities of leaders, including facilitating meetings and sharing ideas on important leadership decisions.

When leaders communicate concisely, either orally or in writing, whatever the context, they are letting others know:

- They have clarity about situations or ideas (which engenders perceptions of competence among those who interact with the leader).
- They are respectful of others' time and will not waste it.
- They value efficiency and prompt response to problems or issues.

Collectively, this approach to communication builds trust as well. For example, principals and other school leaders gain credibility when they minimize administrivia during meetings. Meetings that focus on professional development topics send a powerful message about priorities for staff and student learning.

One forum for communication is the faculty, team, or department meeting. In this context, a school leader can use everyday language with precision to inspire staff members to realize the organization's mission. Sometimes this involves storytelling, as in the following example:

Our student population has dramatically changed in these last two years. Because of changes in our demographics, 65 percent of our students are now English language learners (ELLs). Our staff has risen to the challenge by learning about strategies to teach ELLs. The staff has begun a "word of the day" program, collegial tutoring, parent outreach effort, student recognition assemblies . . . and we are reaping the fruits of our labors! A young man who spoke no English two years ago has been named salutatorian. I celebrate each and every one of you for your contribution to his success!

Such communications send powerful, concrete messages about a leader's values, support for realizing the vision and mission, recognition of effort, and priorities.

A meeting's focus and content should reflect the messages that school leaders wish to convey to constituents. For example, one principal, emphasizing the moral responsibility every staff member has for student success, opened each meeting, every newsletter, and every e-mail bulletin with success stories told by teachers or paraprofessionals and illustrated with student work.

Related activities to communicate this vital connection between staff effort and student learning include asking staff members to brainstorm and list qualities and characteristics of great teachers from their past. Staff members compare and contrast their lists. The final task involves asking staff to commit to modeling these qualities and characteristics in their own work with students.

Teacher leaders at one school opened a faculty meeting by showing a DVD excerpt from the movie *Mr. Holland's Opus* in which Mr. Holland was celebrated by former students who surprised him by playing his composition *The American Symphony.* Then the teacher leaders asked their colleagues to write about the legacy they each wanted to leave students. These were shared publicly both in the faculty meeting and at Back to School Night, attended by parents and guardians, community members, and students. There was not a dry eye in the house!

One superintendent begins every principals meeting with a success story from the district. He follows the story with an activity in which principals engage, and then they make plans to implement a particular idea with faculty colleagues at their respective school sites. For example, at one meeting, the superintendent shared four different articles about teaching students skills that will enable them to thrive in the 21st century. Principals sat in groups of four, each group member reading a different article. After the articles had been read, principals shared key points and talked about the implications for curriculum content, delivery, and assessment. Then they addressed how they could implement the same learning experience in their school buildings with staff. Reflecting on the activity, the superintendent said, "I want my words, actions, and use of time to communicate the value I place on learning at all levels. At the same time I communicate this, I am also communicating a strategy for capacity building." This leader's words and deeds are reminiscent of Lincoln's. Just as Lincoln viewed communication as a tool to express his position, it also contributed to his enduring legacy, which influenced policy and practice in years to come.

Lincoln was a storyteller. As mentioned earlier in this chapter, Lincoln used story and metaphor for a variety of purposes. For example, to illustrate the importance of practice and perseverance, Lincoln shared with the Reverend John Gulliver a brief story about his childhood obsession with acquiring knowledge and comprehending new ideas. Lincoln used metaphor when he compared the venomous snake to the expansion of slavery. During the darkest days of the war, when some influential bank presidents questioned Lincoln as to whether the Union would survive, he characteristically made his point with a story that illustrated his steadfast belief in the viability of the Union:

> "When I was a young man in Illinois," he said, "I boarded for a time with a deacon of the Presbyterian church. One night I was aroused from my sleep by a rap on the door, and I heard the deacon's voice exclaiming, 'Arise Abraham! The day of judgment has come!' I sprang from my bed and rushed to the window, and saw the stars falling in great showers; but looking back of them in the heavens I saw the grand old constellations, with which I was so well acquainted, fixed and true in their places. Gentlemen, the world did not come to an end then, nor will the Union now." (Whitman, 1892/1964, Vol. II, p. 537)

Interestingly, research on leadership indicates that storytelling can be a valuable leadership tool to give meaning and to shape the mission, vision, and direction of an organization. Gardner (1995) suggests that "a key—perhaps the key—to leadership as well as to garnering of a following, is the effective communication of a story. . . . The most fundamental stories fashioned by leaders concern issues of personal and group identity" (p. 62). To illustrate, a middle school principal in South Carolina shared the following story with her staff:

I was a high school dropout. I was one of those kids who just slipped through the cracks. I perceived that none of my teachers seemed to believe in me. I said I didn't care. But I did. In fact, it hurt. I later got my GED and went on to college. Because of my personal experience, I am deeply committed to making our school a haven for every student. Together, we will provide safety nets so that no student will be left adrift or fall through the cracks.

The staff listened intently, many in disbelief. And they behaved differently after they heard the principal's story. The talk in the hallways, the parking lot, and the teachers room was about teaching, learning, and problem-solving difficult cases to foster student learning. The principal's personal resolve galvanized action to make a difference in students' lives. It fostered change. In *Leading Minds: An Anatomy of Leadership*, Gardner (1995) argues that

> The story is a basic human cognitive form; the artful creation and articulation of stories constitutes a fundamental part of the leader's vocation. Stories speak to both parts of the human mind—its reason and emotion. And I suggest, further, that it is *stories of identity*—narratives that help individuals think about and feel who they are, where they come from, and where they are headed—that constitute the single most powerful weapon in the leader's literary arsenal. (p. 43)

In their classic book, *The Leadership Challenge*, Kouzes and Posner (2002) make a compelling argument for storytelling as a leadership tool. Here are some of their reflections:

- "Think of yourself as the chief historian of your team." (p. 100)
- "Telling great stories is one of the most effective ways leaders can model the values and beliefs essential to organizational success." (p. 381)
- "Well-told stories reach inside us and pull us along." (p. 383)

Lincoln used anecdotes to lend clarity to important ideas and to connect emotionally with an audience. To illustrate, in the previously mentioned 1860 Cooper Union address, Lincoln compared the Southern threat to leave the Union to the hypocrisy of a highwayman who tells an innocent robbery victim that if he did not cooperate he would be responsible for his own death. Lincoln's anecdotes, stories, and metaphorical references helped to crystallize ideas for the audience and generated support for his ideals. In a similar way, leaders who capitalize on storytelling communicate a sincerity about the quest to accomplish treasured organizational goals and generate action to do so.

Just as the language of story draws people in, fostering, in many contexts, a closeness, words also have the capacity to alienate. For example, when staff members use acronyms or jargon unfamiliar to a parent, community member, or newcomer to the organization, it sends a strong message that "you're not one of us." A parent remarked, "After hearing the teacher say RTI should provide support for the IEP of this child so let's bring that up at the next CST meeting, I felt like I was swimming in alphabet soup!" School leaders who are sensitive to the subtle messages of language are careful to avoid jargon and issues that may be offensive in multicultural settings. They are able to communicate in a way that is informed by a perspective of what the listener may be perceiving.

As we noted earlier, Lincoln's use of language appealed to a wide audience because his words conveyed a clear message based on concrete ideas, interspersed with metaphor, story, and figurative language. Leaders who follow similar practices are able to communicate succinctly and credibly with a spectrum of organizational members—from bus drivers and cafeteria workers to the superintendent or director of schools. In doing so, these leaders are able to communicate the vision of the organization at all levels and, consequently, influence how students are treated by every individual with whom they interact. These leaders' words often paint pictures in both written and oral form.

Leaders adept at communication also value—and dedicate themselves to creating—environments where information flows easily. They work diligently to create structures that facilitate two-way conversations about teaching, learning, and data. School cultures that function as professional learning communities are one example of this. These schools have institutionalized forums for professional dialogue that focus on results. Communication in this type of context is indeed a two-way street.

As Lincoln's example attests, effective communicators place great value on feedback to ascertain whether they have derived a desired effect. For instance, the remarkable final paragraph of the First Inaugural Address was a reflection of feedback solicited from Secretary of State William Seward. Similarly, Lincoln read newspapers voraciously and used the feedback and criticism from the papers to gauge his public standing. After refining his position, Lincoln would articulate his ideas by writing letters to newspapers. The famous August 1862 letter to Horace Greeley, the editor of the *New York Tribune*, is an example.

Skillful school leaders constantly seek feedback about the effectiveness of their actions. In environments where the cultural norms support rigorous examination of communications and their consequences, leaders and other organizational members grow and refine their practices, increasing their effectiveness. This feedback can occur in several contexts: during peer-to-peer interactions related to teaching and learning, during supervisory visits, during professional learning days, on surveys, and in informal conversations. To cultivate norms that support these conversations, school leaders must be visible, be open, emphasize that dialogue and reflection are actually more powerful in many cases than an observation, request and honor feedback, and portray the invitation for feedback in a sincere manner. Seeking feedback also has a humbling effect. It conveys to organizational members that we are all "good but growing" and allows the leader to model the role of "leader as learner."

Lincoln faced the challenge of communicating with a broad array of his constituency by prospecting the media of the day: telegraph and newspapers. He communicated with and listened to the public. Similarly, school leaders must also prospect the media of the day to maximize the flow of information from the school or district to the larger community—and in the other direction as well. Contemporary leaders use a combination of print, electronic communication, and social networking. Yet successful leaders realize that although Internet-based forms of communication—e-mail, Web sites, and blogs—can be powerful and far-reaching, they often lack the personal touch afforded by face-to-face communication. One whole dimension of communication—the ability to read and respond to the body language of listeners—is missing with electronic formats. Telling stories and using metaphors, analogies, and figurative language can, however, diminish this gap. What the Internet can provide is on-demand responses to inquiries from parents, students, and community members. A teacher's online homework page and tutoring assistance are examples.

Finally, skillful school leaders are great listeners. They "listen" to data from all levels of the organization and use this information to respond with understanding. By listening first and assessing the situation before speaking, school leaders show respect for the speaker and can more accurately analyze and respond appropriately. On some occasions, this strategy diminishes the emotions attached to a situation, gives the person speaking the "space in time" to present the facts, and provides "think time" for the leader. One morning, for instance, an angry parent got out of her car and approached a principal who was greeting students as they got off the bus. "I need to have a word with you!" she snapped. The principal suggested they go to the office, walking briskly until they reached the conference room. The principal stated, "This will be a more comfortable room [in which] to meet." The angry parent continued, "I'm going to kick that bus driver's a__! I dropped my son off at Sumner Avenue. My son was at the corner, walking to the bus stop. The bus driver was at the stop and saw him. My son started running to the stop, and the bus driver pulled away from the curb and left! What kind of concern does he have for kids anyway?" The principal listened intently, silently taking notes. Her silence seemed to defuse some of the parent's anger. "Let me see if I've written down all the facts related to this incident," the principal said. She reiterated what the parent had communicated and then said, "I'll contact the transportation supervisor." "You can," said the parent, "but I've already called and reamed him [out]! I don't know what good that would do." The principal listened and then responded, "I understand your concern for your son. I know your call to the transportation supervisor was made when you were upset. I will speak to the supervisor and get back to you." The parent retorted, "Do what you wish. I just don't want my son to be left again."

When the parent left, the principal called the transportation supervisor. He was out of the office, so she left a message. Meanwhile, the parent drove to the bus yard, where she encountered the supervisor. She approached him and introduced herself. He interrupted her, pointing his finger at her, and said, "You listen to me. I run a tight ship. Our buses must keep to their schedules. If we waited a minute for every child who was almost at a stop, we'd get all the kids to school late. I'm not making an exception for you!" The parent interrupted him and said, "I was going to apologize and try to talk with you. I see you have no interest in that. I'll communicate about this situation with the board members instead. And I promise you, this ain't going to be pretty!"

As the first part of this scenario conveys, when a leader listens and expresses interest, as the principal did, progress toward resolving issues is facilitated. On the other hand, when a leader responds in anger instead of listening, as the transportation supervisor did, the situation is exacerbated. The ability of leaders to manage their emotions and look at a situation from another's perspective is essential to resolving conflict. Conversely, failure to behave empathetically invites friction and precipitates conflict.

In addition to listening, another silent communication tool is available. Dr. Kent Peterson, professor of educational administration at the University of Wisconsin, often says, "What you do speaks so loudly I cannot hear what you say!" Consider the message conveyed when a superintendent pulls principals out of a professional development session on "Supervising Teaching to Promote Student Learning" to talk about the budget. Or what is the message communicated when a principal introduces a keynote speaker and says to the audience, "This is going to be great!" and then walks out? As the cliché states, actions speak louder than words.

Having reached this point in the chapter, readers might ponder the following questions:

- What messages about communication has this chapter conveyed?
- What have I learned about Lincoln's practices that will influence my own legacy and the legacy I will leave for tomorrow's leaders?

Reflecting on History and the Moment: Implications for the Future

Precision in language, clarity, and the capacity to make an emotional connection with an audience were intentional communication strategies that Lincoln sought to develop and refine throughout his life. He solicited feedback from others and used experimentation and reflection to assess whether his words matched his intentions. School leaders who are able to communicate ideas with clarity, in everyday language, in ways that foster emotional connections, have an edge in accomplishing their goals. Their daily interactions with individuals at all levels of the organization are crystal clear and motivate others to stay the course. They constantly seek feedback from self and others to determine if their communications have their intended effects.

The following table is designed as a tool for reflection and future action. Use it to illuminate the way on your future leadership journey.

Reflecting on Communication and Its Impact		
Lincoln's Example	Evidence If Example Is Successfully Modeled	Current Assessment of My Performance
Crisp and concise writing		
Use of language understood by everyone; use of metaphors, stories to enhance understanding		
Seeking and using feedback		
Mastering various forms of media		
Patient listening		
Actions aligning with words		

According to Kouzes and Posner (2002), stories do the following:

- Put a human face on success.
- Tell us that someone like us can make a difference.
- Create organizational role models that we can relate to.

- Put behavior in an authentic context.
- Make standards more than statistics.
- Provide detail to understand the culture.

In addition, stories help leaders address different situations through analogy. Think of a message you would like to communicate, or perhaps a problem you wish to solve. Create or construct a story in the space below. Then tell your story to a trusted colleague and ask for feedback. Revise your story accordingly.

Now reflect on what matters most to you personally and in your work as a leader, using the following questions as a guide.

- What is it that you want to communicate in your daily work with others?

• Are your words, stories, use of language, analogies, and metaphors in alignment, or is it time to write to order your thoughts and realign them so that your expression has greater dignity?

• What is the legacy you have been inspired to leave?

Use this space to jot down any other ideas, insights, or new perspectives from this chapter that you wish to add to your repertoire as a school leader.

CHAPTER THREE

Building a Diverse and Competent Team to Successfully Address the Mission

[Lincoln] also understood something else. He recognized that while each of us must do our part, work as hard as we can, and be as responsible as we can—although we are responsible for our own fates, in the end, there are certain things we cannot do on our own. There are certain things we can only do together. There are certain things only a union can do.

—President Barack Obama,
on the 200th anniversary of the birth of
President Lincoln, February 12, 2009

Lincoln knew that his inexperience as a national leader would be a hurdle during the initial stages of his presidency (Donald, 1995). He lacked the executive experience to lead the federal government, assist the military, support the treasury, and negotiate foreign policy. Fortunately, he recognized the executive and knowledge-based qualities of those he had defeated for the nomination and decided to bring those individuals into his cabinet regardless of their personal ambitions and jealousies. He believed it was best for the nation to bring the brightest and most experienced on board. Although his relationship with many of these leaders was difficult at times, his strategy, *based on results*, worked. These partnerships enabled Lincoln to tap into the rich expertise needed to pursue the national mission and vision. As noted in Chapter 2, the writing partnership between Secretary Seward and President

Lincoln on the First Inaugural Address is a good example of how working together can benefit the mission.

This lesson is critical for school leaders. DuFour and Eaker (1998) note, "Without collaborative processes that foster ownership in decisions, schools will not generate the shared commitments and results orientation of a learning community" (p. 153). Lincoln's example of bringing aboard individuals with diverse personalities, ideas, and ambitions sheds light on the value of separating person from practice and choosing competence over personality.

Drawing on the Talents of Others

Lincoln's success in securing the Republican presidential nomination in May 1860 indicated that using a diverse team to accomplish his goals was a practice he believed in even before becoming president. White (2009) notes that tradition has created the notion that Lincoln was his own campaign manager in 1860 and secured the nomination by his own design. This is untrue. Lincoln secured the nomination by coordinating the efforts of a wide variety of advisors. "Lincoln's genius was his ability to draw upon the talents of others, meld together diverse personalities who often did not trust one another, and then listen to their advice, recognizing that it was sometimes wiser than his own" (White, 2009, p. 319). Interestingly, at times Lincoln thought it necessary to coordinate the team effort without necessarily bringing all the team members together. Of course, in 1860 it was more difficult to bring people together than it is today, simply because of transportation limitations. But even when in the White House, with all cabinet members in Washington, Lincoln often worked with his team as individuals, to accomplish group goals.

On November 7, 1860, the day after he was elected president, Lincoln "resolved . . . to surround himself with the strongest men from every faction of the new Republican Party—former Whigs, Free-Soilers, and antislavery Democrats" (Goodwin, 2005, p. 280). The three major personalities that Lincoln would have to work with in his cabinet were War Secretary Edwin Stanton (who replaced Simon Cameron in January 1862), Treasury Secretary Salmon Chase, and Secretary of State William Seward. All three men had a far greater chance than Lincoln of securing the Republican presidential nomination in 1860 and thought their skills were superior to the president's—but now they were working for the one-term Illinois congressman and lawyer.

Stanton's history and relationship with Lincoln were especially intriguing. Back in 1855, Lincoln was expected to serve as cocounsel with Stanton on the celebrated McCormick Reaper patent case in Cincinnati, Ohio. At the time, Stanton was a nationally known and respected Pennsylvania lawyer. Although much respected for his work within the Eighth Judicial Circuit, Lincoln was relatively unknown for his law work beyond Illinois. With a passion for inventions and new mechanical gadgets, he prepared extensively for the case and looked forward to working with Stanton. (Lincoln, interestingly, had applied for a patent in 1849 for a device he designed to help keep boats afloat over sandbars and shoals.) Stanton, however, viewed Lincoln "as a Western hick and snubbed him throughout the trial . . . [and] supposedly referred to him as 'that giraffe' and that 'creature from Illinois'" (Oates, 1977, p. 103). Always the lifetime learner, Lincoln remained in the courtroom and learned much from Stanton's performance. Seven years later, on January 13, 1862, Lincoln appointed Stanton to the secretary of war position in his cabinet. Stanton was

> astonished that Lincoln had appointed him Secretary of War. After all, Stanton had humiliated Lincoln back in the McCormick Reaper case. And in Washington this past year, Stanton had vilified this "imbecilic" President, this "original gorilla." . . . But Lincoln made it clear that he bore Stanton no ill will. If the McCormick Reaper episode had been one of the most humiliating episodes of his life, Lincoln had put that aside now. He never carried a grudge, he said later, because it didn't pay. (Oates, 1977, p. 278)

Stanton's appointment was another example of Lincoln's greatness; he did not let petty differences serve as obstacles to the greater good. As the nation's leader, Lincoln had an objective to fill the cabinet with those most able to carry out the national purpose—to preserve the Union and to remain a democracy of, by, and for the people. In *Team of Rivals*, Doris Kearns Goodwin (2005) observes that "Lincoln's choice of Stanton would reveal . . . a singular ability to transcend personal vendetta, humiliation, or bitterness. As for Stanton . . . he would . . . come to respect and love Lincoln more than any person outside of his immediate family" (p. 175). When Lincoln died on April 15, 1865, at 7:22 a.m., it was Stanton who stated the immortal words, "Now he belongs to the ages" (this Stanton-Lincoln episode is adapted from Robbins and Alvy, 2009, p. 36).

John Hay, Lincoln's personal secretary, once reflected that Lincoln and Stanton worked well together because they "often cancelled out each other's faults" (Thomas, 1952, p. 297). When compared to Stanton, Lincoln had the strengths of openness, forgiveness of mistakes, remaining calm in most situations, and using humor and simplicity; Lincoln needed Stanton's toughness with subordinates, intolerance of mistakes, fiery temper, and preference for formality. Similarly, White (2009) draws interesting contrasts between Secretary of State Seward and the president:

> To other members of Lincoln's cabinet, and many in Washington, Lincoln and Seward were an odd couple. As the two men lounged in Seward's library, the secretary of state would take pleasure in his Havana cigars, while Lincoln did not smoke; Seward enjoyed vintage wines and brandy, while Lincoln did not drink; Seward was known for his colorful language, whereas Lincoln almost never swore. (p. 479)

Almost from the day he took office, Secretary of the Treasury Chase was pining for the Republican presidential nomination in 1864. Lincoln knew this but admired Chase's ability to keep the financial house in order. Lincoln respected Chase's "wizardry" in raising money for the war and thus tolerated Chase's critical views on how the war was managed. Chase would tell confidants that he had little influence with the president and no voice in war-related decision making. Chase especially resented Seward's role and influence with the president on major policy issues. The jealousy and conflict between Chase and Seward came to a head in December 1862, with several Capitol Hill leaders supporting Chase. The leaders shared their views with the president. In the end, both Chase and Seward offered to resign, but the president accepted neither resignation and told a friend that with both men back on board, "I've got a pumpkin in each end of my bag" (Thomas, 1952, pp.

351–354). However, by the time Chase handed in his third resignation letter in June 1864, Lincoln accepted, to Chase's surprise. Most observers thought that Lincoln was finished working with Chase.

Then, in December 1864, Lincoln again proved that he would do what was best for the nation regardless of personal history. Lincoln nominated Salmon Chase as chief justice of the United States Supreme Court. Many Lincoln supporters were shocked by the choice because of the two men's rocky history. To a group of friends who opposed Chase's appointment, Lincoln replied:

> "Mr. Chase is a very able man. He is a very ambitious man and I think on the subject of the presidency a little insane. He has not always behaved very well lately and people say to me, 'Now is the time to *crush him out.*' Well, I'm not in favor of crushing anybody out! If there is anything that a man can do and do it well, I say let him do it. Give him a chance. . . ." On December 6, Lincoln wrote Chase's nomination in his own hand and sent it to the Senate for confirmation, thus honoring his most troublesome antagonist with the highest office he could bestow. (Thomas, 1952, p. 492)

John Nicolay, one of Lincoln's personal secretaries, reacted to the Chase appointment by stating to his fiancée:

> Probably no other man than Lincoln would have had . . . the degree of magnanimity to thus forgive and exalt a rival who had so deeply and so unjustifiably intrigued against him. It is . . . only another most marked illustration of the greatness of the President, in this age of little men. (Donald, 2003, p. 203)

Historian Sean Wilentz (2009) examined the strained relationship between Lincoln and his cabinet members and takes a position contrary to those who believe that Lincoln's cabinet formed a successful team. Wilentz asserts that Lincoln's cabinet was "a dysfunctional collection of schemers far more than it was a team of any kind" (p. 27). Wilentz stresses that Lincoln's great skill was that of a politician who accomplished his goals through political astuteness and know-how. He suggests that since politicians are less respected today than in Lincoln's time, scholars are reluctant to imply that instinctual political skills were a key to Lincoln's success. Although Wilentz's stance is certainly a minority position among Lincoln scholars, it does add a reality check to the "successful team" viewpoint.

Going Solo When Necessary

One should not get the impression that Lincoln always consulted his cabinet, or individual cabinet members, before making a major decision. To illustrate, Lincoln did not consult his cabinet when initially presenting the Emancipation Proclamation to them on July 22, 1862. His draft of the emancipation document completely surprised the team. Lincoln explained that he "had resolved upon this step and had not called them together to ask their advice, but to lay the subject-matter of a proclamation before them" and solicit suggestions (Burlingame, 2008, Vol. 2, p. 363). Although the historical record is a bit unclear concerning which cabinet members supported or opposed the president's proclamation, it is generally agreed that Seward suggested that the president wait before publicly issuing the proclamation until the North could claim an important military victory. That victory, although a limited one, took place at Antietam on September 17, 1862. Lincoln then read a revised draft of the proclamation to his cabinet on September 22, to be formally issued on January 1, 1863.

A More Difficult Talent Search: Finding General Grant

When we assess Lincoln's talent for selecting a diverse and successful team, it is important to address an aspect of Lincoln's "talent search" in which he undoubtedly thought he had failed—finding a leading general who held his vision of what needed to be accomplished on the battlefield. He failed in this regard until his selection of Ulysses Grant in March 1864. Lincoln settled on Grant only 13 months before the end of the war. Before Grant's selection, Generals McClellan, Burnside, Halleck, Hooker, and Meade had all served as top commander of the Union effort. Each choice seemed to make sense at the time. But in Lincoln's opinion, each general failed to take the initiative, use sound strategy, or finish the job. Historians have provided many explanations for Lincoln's inability to select the right military leaders, including one explanation that was beyond his control—top commanders such as Robert E. Lee chose to fight for the Confederacy. Also, because of Lincoln's very limited military experience (six months), he deferred to his generals until he acquired a greater knowledge of military strategy. In *Tried by War*, McPherson (2008a) suggests that

> Lincoln's on-the-job training as commander in chief went through some rough patches. He made mistakes—but he also learned from those mistakes. He deferred too long to McClellan's supposedly superior professional qualifications. Perhaps he should have overruled that general's preference for the Peninsula strategy. . . . In retrospect it appears that he also made several wrong appointments to command the Army of the Potomac. Yet in each case the general he named seemed to be the best man for the job when he was appointed. (p. 266)

The success in Lincoln's selection of cabinet officers, compared to his selection of generals, is puzzling. One explanation might be that Lincoln was able to keep an eye on, and monitor, the daily actions of his cabinet rivals, while it was difficult to keep an immediate tab on his battlefield commanders. Another explanation is that Lincoln instinctively understood politicians and their behavior; learning how generals behaved was a more challenging assignment for someone without military experience. Yet, as a result of analyzing War Department communiqués, meetings with his generals, and weighing the mixed battlefield results Lincoln learned—through a painstakingly slow process—what to look for in a battlefield commander. Out of necessity, as this selection process was occurring, Lincoln became the most active commander in chief in United States history. It was (and continues to be) almost unprecedented for a president to engage in real-time decisions related to military campaigns—yet the times demanded his engagement to carry out the national mission and vision.

In the opening of this chapter we noted that Lincoln recognized his own lack of executive experience. He understood his strengths and weaknesses. An important strategy used by effective leaders is to build on assets, not deficits.

Lincoln looked for the strengths in others and was willing to overlook their frailties to accomplish the greater good. Stanton may have been gruff, but he believed in accountability. Chase may have been too ambitious, but he understood finances. As for Lincoln, he may have been too easy on friends, but he kept his eye on the mission.

Lincoln's Life and Work: Implications for School Leaders

Casey Stengel, the baseball manager, once said, "Getting good players is easy. Getting 'em to play together is the hard part." Lincoln's commitment to build a balanced and diverse team (i.e., expertise, perspective, opinion) to accomplish his goals was a practice he was known for; but as we noted earlier, at times it contributed to an arduous "adventure." Similarly, the work of school leaders has become so incredibly complex that no one person can address the many demands of the role. However, sharing leadership responsibilities is a daunting challenge. The late Kathleen Cotton (2003) wrote:

> A large and growing volume of research repeatedly finds that, when principals empower their staffs, through sharing leadership and decision-making authority with them, everyone benefits, including students. . . . There are simply too many decisions in a typical school for one person to handle effectively. (pp. 21–22)

School leaders work with a plethora of teams, boards, and groups. Individuals on those teams and boards are often the ones with the most knowledge and expertise regarding the types of decisions that will be made, but are often very diverse in terms of personalities and temperaments. Further,

> closely related to the benefits of shared decision making are the researcher's discoveries about the positive outcomes that emerge when principals and others establish and maintain a truly collaborative culture. In such a culture, schooling is "deprivatized," and there is a norm of principal, teachers, and others learning and planning and working together to upgrade their skills and knowledge and improve their school. (Cotton, 2003, p. 23)

The importance of the focus on improvement cannot be overstated. In fact, when interviewed by the National Staff Development Council, Judith Warren Little cautioned:

> I want to really underscore the conceptual neutrality of the term com-munity—there is nothing about community that is necessarily virtuous or improvement oriented. There is certainly evidence throughout history of very strong communities that are up to no good. Strong communities are much better about preserving practice and viewpoint than they are about changing. However, if groups have a disposition to embrace com-munity in pursuit of instructional improvement and to embrace inves-tigation of their own assumptions and practices toward that end, then community can be transformational. (Crow, 2008, p. 54)

For school leaders, these words hold a powerful message. That is, the leader's task is to organize the school or district to support collaborative work, create those conditions that will allow it to occur, and ensure that the col-laboration is purposeful for those involved. For example, leaders can facilitate developing a schedule that creates time for a data team to meet and engage in what team members identify as critical areas of focus. The focus of the work needs to be owned by team members and to create value for their participa-tion. Again, Judith Warren Little's insights are critical: "If working as a com-munity doesn't carry value added over what teachers are able to accomplish independently, then it won't be worth the transactional costs, the investment of time, and the competition with what teachers feel that they have to do individually" (Crow, 2008, p. 54).

Lincoln engaged individuals with specific refined skill sets and rich exper-tise to become members of his cabinet, sharing a common focus: the pur-suit of the national mission and vision. Similarly, school leaders need to engage individual teacher leaders on teams devoted to examining practice and its effect on results—student achievement. Their engagement to this end affects life paths of students, and ultimately the citizens of tomorrow. Lincoln had a unique ability to bring together individuals with diverse personalities, ideas, and ambitions, and he was able to separate person from practice and to choose competence over personality. These abilities required great vision and skillfulness. School leaders often find themselves in a predicament of having to harness the rich expertise of individuals with diverse personalities, motivations, and values. These characteristics can provide for a tumultuous mix unless the joint cause in which they engage is sufficiently challenging and norms are put into place proactively to focus on practice versus person and competence versus personality.

School leaders need a repertoire of skills to structure collaborative work so it is results driven and purposeful for those who engage in it. For example, one school leader routinely begins a team's first meeting with a process she refers to as "doughnut hole norms." Team members are asked to sit around a sheet of butcher paper and draw a huge doughnut with a large hole in the middle. They section off the doughnut into as many parts as there are team members. The team members are instructed to reflect upon those norms for behavior that they, as individuals, wish to abide by in team meetings and write these, without speaking to one another, in their section of the dough-nut. After this is completed, team members read what they have written. Where there is agreement or consensus with an individual's norm, that norm is written in the doughnut hole. When all members have finished their lists and the center list is completed, team members endorse the norms for behav-ior by signing the doughnut. The doughnut becomes a document that influ-ences behavior during team meetings.

School leaders often ask team members to assess their individual and collective personalities as a way to understand their similarities and differ-ences. After doing this, one team member reflected, "The personality style assessment helped me realize that I was a 'task first, relationship second' type of personality, whereas many of my colleagues on the team were 'relation-ship first, task second.' I needed to understand this to comprehend why they perceived I was abrupt and to the point—and didn't take time for being 'all cordial'!" As Marzano and colleagues attest,

> A case can be made that effective professional relationships are central to the effective execution of many of the other [20] responsibilities. In the context of our meta-analysis, the responsibility of *Relationships* refers to the extent to which the school leader demonstrates an awareness of the personal lives of teachers and staff. (2005, p. 58)

School leaders may infer from this observation that attending to developing technical skills like creating norms among team members and facilitating the understanding of personalities is not enough. To make a real difference in productivity, they must also develop a foundation of congeniality and trust, as well as recognize teacher effort. Attention to this level of detail has its rewards. The team becomes greater than the sum of its parts.

Jon Katzenbach and Douglas Smith (1993) define *team* as "a small number of people with complementary skills who are committed to a common purpose, set of performance goals, and approach for which they hold themselves mutually accountable" (p. 111). To function as an effective team, it is essential that team members take time to talk about the purpose of their work and how to do the work rather than leaving those details to chance. They need to spend time building trust, rapport, and relationships with each other. Katzenbach and Smith also specify that not all groups are teams. For example, teams are characterized as having shared leadership roles, whereas working groups often have a strong, visibly focused leader. Teams generate collective work products, whereas working groups produce individual work. Teams measure their effectiveness by evaluating collective work products; working groups measure their effectiveness indirectly by its influence on others, such as students' learning goals.

Despite the expertise that individual team members bring to the table, as they begin to work closely with one another, values may clash and tempers may begin to flare. Tuckman's (1965) classic article documents that most teams go through a fairly predictable evolution from a "forming," polite stage, wherein members get to know one another; then a "storming" stage, characterized by infighting and conflict; followed by a "norming" stage, during which team members develop collaborative skills; and finally a "performing" stage, wherein relationships among team members are close and supportive and the work they do is effective. Later, Tuckman added a fifth stage, "adjourning," in which team members assess their work, close one project, and renew ideas for the next group enterprise (Smith, 2005). As you examine Tuckman's model (see Figure 3.1, p. 51), think about the teams in your organization and ponder the following questions:

- At what stage are they functioning?
- What logical next steps might they take to achieve maturity?

Being aware of what stage a team is at can help school leaders identify the level and type of support team members need to arrive at the performing and adjourning stages.

Just as Lincoln relied on others for leadership expertise related to specific functions, "surround[ing] himself with some of the largest and most self-regarding talents in the party" (Carwardine, 2006, pp. 152–154), school principals realize that they cannot single-handedly take on all or even most of the leadership roles in the building. Linda Lambert (1998) defines leadership capacity as "broad-based, skillful participation in the work of leadership . . . involving attention to shared learning that leads to shared purpose and action" (p. 91). She suggests that "high leadership capacity" includes five critical features:

- Broad-based, skillful participation in the work of leadership.
- Inquiry-based use of information to inform shared decisions and practice.
- Roles and responsibilities that reflect broad involvement and collaboration.
- Reflective practice/innovation as the norm.
- High student achievement. (pp. 16–17)

Without broad-based participation, improvement efforts will likely fail. School leaders who bring together the people closest to the "product" (student learning) and develop their skillfulness in enhancing the collective capacity of the staff to foster learning can accomplish more than leaders in schools where staff members function in isolation. By emphasizing relationship building and professional community and enhancing the skillfulness of organizational members, these school leaders are able to capture the rich expertise of individuals and bind them together in collaborative teams where their individual talents complement one another within learning cultures that encompass the wisdom of many.

Figure 3.1

Tuckman's Stages of Team Development

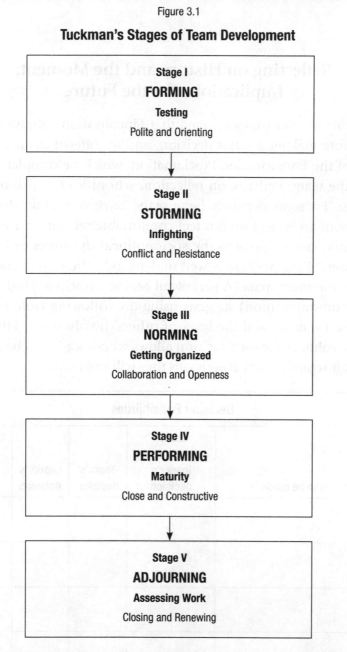

Stage I
FORMING
Testing
Polite and Orienting

Stage II
STORMING
Infighting
Conflict and Resistance

Stage III
NORMING
Getting Organized
Collaboration and Openness

Stage IV
PERFORMING
Maturity
Close and Constructive

Stage V
ADJOURNING
Assessing Work
Closing and Renewing

Source: Adapted from 12MANAGE The Executive Fast Track. www.12manage.com. © 12Manage.com. Adapted with permission. Stages of team development (B. Tuckman). *The Executive Fast Track*. Retrieved October 14, 2009, from http://www.12manage. com/methods_tuckman_stages_team_development.html

Reflecting on History and the Moment: Implications for the Future

Earlier in this chapter we mentioned that Lincoln didn't always consult his cabinet before making a major decision, and we offered as an example the first draft of the Emancipation Proclamation, which he completed and presented to the team. Perhaps, on reflection, school leaders will have a view such as this: "For some decisions, because the 'buck stops at my door' or I feel strongly about an issue, I do not feel comfortable relying on a team whose members may not be privy to the sociopolitical dynamics or background of a situation." Your position is well understood! There are some decisions that you alone must make. A successful Maine principal, Linda Gaidimas (personal communication) suggests using the following table to delineate decisions to be made and the level of others' involvement. Filling in the appropriate columns for each decision allows school leaders to be transparent with the staff regarding which decisions they will influence.

Decision Possibilities				
Decision to be made	Leader consults team; leader's decision	Team's decision	Leader's decision	Collaborative decision (team and leader)

When thinking about team membership, consider that for survival reasons we often make quick decisions about the intentions of others toward us based on our perceptions of their warmth and competence. Harvard researcher Amy Cuddy (2009), summarizing the psychological research involving thousands of subjects, suggests that

> inevitably, of course, we find clues to warmth and competence in stereotypes based on people's race, gender, or nationality. Thus, many of our decisions about whom to trust, doubt, attack, defend, hire, or fire, are based on faulty data. . . . [Further, research demonstrates that] people tend to see warmth and competence as inversely related. If there's an apparent surplus of one trait, they infer a deficit of the other. (p. 24)

In other words, if people appear kind, they are often perceived as inept or less competent in a workplace context. So how can school leaders use this information as well as Lincoln's example of including in his cabinet those he defeated to construct high-performing teams and retain high-quality employees? First, be aware of Cuddy's research and reflect on Lincoln's cabinet example. Second, realize that warmth and competence are two separate dimensions. Recognize that one's positive social skills play a critical role in team functioning and customer service. Assess these traits objectively when forming a team. Then identify the essential roles that are needed for the team (or cabinet) to function well and the requisite behaviors for these roles. Thinking about the larger vision or mission first, and focusing on that as an outcome, then selecting individuals who collectively contribute both the hard and soft skills to realize the vision will serve this purpose well. Both competence and passion, character and skillfulness, will be harnessed for school success. Consider these issues while reflecting on the following questions:

- What is the vision or mission we wish to pursue with the team?

• What are the individual qualities of team members that would serve the team well?

• If team members differ in personalities, expertise, or years of experience, how might this contribute positively to team functioning and to realizing the vision? How might these differences pose a challenge to team functioning and trust building? How might we plan proactively to overcome this potential stumbling block?

• What personality traits or behaviors "push my buttons" as a leader? How can I be mindful of this and put the vision first when making critical decisions about team or cabinet membership? If the team or cabinet is already formed, how can this self-knowledge and the knowledge of Lincoln's example be combined to fuel my capacity to work productively with diverse team members?

Use this space to jot down any other ideas, insights, or new perspectives from this chapter that you wish to add to your repertoire as a school leader.

CHAPTER FOUR

Engendering Trust, Loyalty, and Respect Through Humility, Humor, and Personal Example

> Competence counts. But what ultimately distinguishes the great leaders from the mediocre are the personal inner qualities—qualities that are hard to define but are essential for success, qualities that each of us must develop for ourselves . . ."
>
> —David Gergen in *True North*, by Bill George, p. xvii

The research on leadership is clear: personal example is the most powerful human resource available to lead an organization. In the case of Abraham Lincoln, it was his personal behavior, his character, his story that have brought so many individuals, worldwide, to the study of his life. As Russian novelist Leo Tolstoy said, "His example is universal and will last thousands of years . . . and as a great character he will live as long as the world lives" (quoted from *The World*, 1909, in Goodwin, 2005, p. ix).

Zenger and Folkman (2002) conclude that "everything about great leaders radiates from character (p. ix), and Kouzes and Posner (2002) remind us to "model the way," "[since] your behavior . . . wins you respect" (p. 14). And, of course, respect and trust go hand in hand. Building trust is critical for leaders at every level to accomplish organizational goals. Tschannen-Moran (2004), in *Trust Matters*, states that

> effective school leaders not only know how to "talk the talk" of trust, they also know how to "walk the walk." If *being a role model* is ever necessary, it's when it comes to cultivating a culture of trust. Discontinuity

between word and example will quickly erode a principal's ability to lead. Setting an example is not to be flaunted. Skillful principals often earn the trust of their faculty by leading quietly. They are soft on people but hard on projects. They combine personal humility—exercising restraint and modesty—with tenacity and the professional will to see that the task is accomplished and accomplished well. (pp. 177–178; emphasis added)

In this chapter we examine Lincoln's behavior to gain a greater understanding of his character. Because leadership research and common sense affirm that character is critical to success, studying the character of a successful leader who faced challenges more overwhelming than anyone of us could imagine will help leaders at every level consider qualities and skills that can improve performance. However, as noted in the introduction of this book, leaders must find their own paths to success, based on their own contexts. Our goal is to help you examine qualities to consider on the personal journey to effective leadership. The qualities examined in this chapter—based on Lincoln's life—include setting a personal example; behaving with humility; engendering trust, loyalty, and respect; and using humor at appropriate times.

The Power of Personal Example and Humility

Frederick Douglass had three meetings with President Lincoln. The following incident, described by Douglass, is a testament to the genuine respect that evolved between the two men during the war, although they deeply disagreed on many issues (Oakes, 2007). The incident also provides us with a glimpse into Lincoln's character and humility. On this occasion Douglass and Lincoln met at a reception following Lincoln's second inauguration, on March 4, 1865. It should be noted that Douglass initially was barred by two policemen from entering the White House because of his color. Douglass then recognized someone who was going to attend the reception and asked, "Be so kind as to say to Mr. Lincoln that Frederick Douglass is detained by officers at the door" (Burlingame, 2008, Vol. 2, p. 769). Within a minute Douglass was ushered in to see the president. Douglass later recalled the events:

I could not have been more than ten feet from him when Mr. Lincoln saw me; his countenance lighted up, and he said in a voice which was heard all around: "Here comes my friend Douglass." As I approached him he reached out his hand, gave me a cordial shake and said: "Douglass, I saw you in the crowd to-day listening to my inaugural address. There is no man's opinion that I value more than yours: what do you think of it?" I said: "Mr. Lincoln, I cannot stop here to talk with you, as there are thousands waiting to shake you by the hand;" but he said again: "What did you think of it?" I said: "Mr. Lincoln, it was a sacred effort," and then I walked off. "I am glad you liked it," he said. (quoted from *Life and Times of Frederick Douglass*, 1881, in Burlingame, 2008, Vol. 2, pp. 769–770)

Interestingly, this encounter between Lincoln and Frederick Douglass also reveals a less obvious beneficial effect of humility: "Humility will make you approachable" (Zenger & Folkman, 2002, p. 234). Individual, collegial, or team humility helps to build relationships and enables individuals and teams to reveal their vulnerabilities and raise issues that might otherwise be "nondiscussables." The opposite of humility, arrogance, steers individuals away from the team. Bill George (2007) tells a story of a rising CEO, Kevin Sharer, who learned the hard way that too much self-assurance turns others off: "I learned that whether you are right or not, there is a price to be paid for arrogance" (p. 36). Carwardine (2006), in his award-winning biography, *Lincoln: A Life of Purpose and Power*, draws the following conclusion: "Most of those who dealt with Lincoln recognized a political confidence that never spilled over, through vanity or a misplaced dignity, into arrogance or self-glorification" (p. 311).

Trust, Loyalty, and Respect

Examples of engendering trust, loyalty, and respect through humility percolate throughout Lincoln's presidency. As we examine these examples, it is important to consider that humility can sometimes be misunderstood as weakness of character because, for example, one is willing to admit mistakes or reluctant to take credit for specific decisions. "A Lincolnesque leader is confident enough to be humble—to not feel the need to bluster or dominate, but to be sufficiently sure of one's own judgment and self-worth to really listen and not be threatened by contrary advice" (Thomas & Wolffe, 2008, pp. 30–31). Consider how trust, loyalty, and respect are displayed in the following examples.

On February 11, 1861, Lincoln departed from Springfield for Washington to assume the presidency in March. He had moved to Springfield in 1837, at the age of 28. At the railroad station, he said the following during his emotional farewell:

> My friends—No one, not in my situation, can appreciate my feeling of sadness at this parting. To this place, and the kindness of these people, I owe every thing. Here I have lived a quarter of a century, and have passed from a young to an old man. Here my children have been born, and one is buried. I now leave, not knowing when, or whether ever, I may return, with a task before me greater than that which rested upon Washington. Without the assistance of that Divine Being, who ever attended him, I cannot succeed. With that assistance I cannot fail. Trusting in Him, who can go with me, and remain with you and be everywhere for good, let us confidently hope that all will yet be well. To His care commending you, as I hope in your prayers you will commend me, I bid you an affectionate farewell. (Basler, 1953–1955, Vol. IV, p. 190)

Burlingame (2008) states that Lincoln spent about 30 minutes saying farewells to Springfield friends, and the occasion was solemn, with Lincoln visibly touched by the expressions of support and love. Lincoln was "trembling with suppressed emotion and radiating profound sadness" (Burlingame, 2008, Vol. 1, p. 759). After Lincoln spoke, there were tears all around, including those of the president-elect. Many in the crowd shouted their support and lifted their hats to honor Lincoln as the train departed. Trust, loyalty, and respect—"To this place and the kindness of these people, I owe every thing." This brief farewell speech reveals Lincoln's unique ability to use common language and touch the heart of an audience. No one in the audience could have missed his love of Springfield, how the community had shaped him, and his debt to the people. Yet he also implied that without their future support, he would fail. A relationship of trust does not end.

In another example of trust, loyalty, and respect, Lincoln revealed in a letter to Ulysses Grant that he had unwisely misjudged the general's military tactics during the capture of Vicksburg on July 4, 1863. What is interesting about this incident is that Lincoln and Grant had not yet met. But, from afar, Lincoln displayed qualities that surely endeared him to the man who would eventually command all Union armies. The letter was written on July 13:

> I do not remember that you and I ever met personally. I write this now as a grateful acknowledgment for the almost inestimable service you have done the country. I wish to say a word further. . . . When you got below, and took Port-Gibson, Grand Gulf, and vicinity, I thought you should go down the river and join Gen. Banks; and when you turned Northward East of the Big Black, I feared it was a mistake. I now wish to make the personal acknowledgment that you were right, and I was wrong.
>
> Yours very truly,
> A. Lincoln
> (Basler, 1953–1955, Vol. VI, p. 326)

How often are leaders willing to say or state in writing, "You were right and I was wrong"? It is a simple phrase, but one that tells a great deal about the president and how he wanted to relate to associates. He was sending a strong message to Grant that they needed to be frank and honest with each other. Interestingly, one of the president's associates was upset because Grant had paroled the Confederate troops who surrendered at Vicksburg. Lincoln took the parole in stride and was unwilling to criticize Grant. Lincoln's magnanimous attitude concerning the parole foreshadows the "malice toward none" theme of the Second Inaugural Address, which we examine in the next chapter. Concerning Lincoln's character, Wills (1992) states, in his Pulitzer Prize–winning book *Lincoln at Gettysburg*, "Lincoln's distinctive mark, one almost unique in the history of war leadership, was his refusal to indulge in triumphalism, righteousness, or vilification of the foe" (p. 183).

Even with his greatest triumph beyond preserving the Union, the emancipation of the slaves, Lincoln was unwilling to take personal credit. In a fascinating letter to the newspaper editor Albert Hodges on April 4, 1864, Lincoln described his thinking on the primary issue of the day:

> I am naturally anti-slavery. If slavery is not wrong, nothing is wrong. I can not remember when I did not so think, and feel. And yet I have never understood that the Presidency conferred upon me an unrestricted right to act officially upon this judgment and feeling. . . . I did understand however, that my oath to preserve the constitution to the best of my ability, imposed upon me the duty of preserving, by every indispensable means, that government—that nation—of which that constitution was the organic law. Was it possible to lose the nation, and yet preserve the constitution? By general law life *and* limb must be protected; yet often a limb must be amputated to save a life; but a life is never wisely given to save a limb . . . and I was, in my best judgment, driven to the alternative of either surrendering the Union, and with it, the Constitution, or of laying strong hand upon the colored element. I chose the latter. . . . In telling this tale I attempt no compliment to my own sagacity. I claim not to have controlled events, but confess plainly that events have controlled me. . . . God alone can claim it. (Basler, 1953–1955, Vol. VII, pp. 281–282)

Here Lincoln addresses several issues. Although he personally opposed slavery, he admits to being a reluctant liberator. In his view, circumstances forced the events. Also, he is unwilling to be credited with wisdom, with sagacity; he seems to be saying that common sense would have led any Union president to make similar decisions. And Lincoln is admitting that even the president of the United States cannot control events; he may have liberated the slaves and recruited tens of thousands of black Americans to serve the Northern war effort, but he maintains that circumstances forced his hand. Finally, he believes that it is God's will, and not the will of man, that will determine the results of the conflict. Lincoln takes no credit; again, triumphalism is absent from this letter.

In October 1863, Lincoln penned a letter to an officer, James Cutts, who had been disciplined primarily because of his unpredictable temper. The advice provides insight into the president's temperament:

> Quarrel not at all. No man resolved to make the most of himself, can spare time for personal contention. Still less can he afford to take all the consequences, including the vitiating of his temper, and the loss of self-control. . . . Better give your path to a dog, than be bitten by him in contesting for the right. Even killing the dog would not cure the bite. (Basler, 1953–1955, Vol. VI, p. 538)

This letter provides some insight into why Lincoln was so successful with managing his cabinet. He suggests that if one wastes time on "personal contention," little will be accomplished. We squander positive and productive actions when we wallow in anger and revenge. Again, Lincoln gained respect because he showed respect for others, even under trying conditions. Recall Lincoln's decision to nominate Salmon Chase to the Supreme Court; if anger had prevailed, the appointment could not have been made. When important issues need to be resolved, holding grudges and losing self-control will only hurt one's mission, damage relationships, and, most important, reduce the opportunity for success.

Humor, Timing, and Sending a Message

Lincoln's sense of humor and ability to reduce the tension in a room is another formidable leadership characteristic. Changing the emotional barometer in a room can sometimes lead to a breakthrough during a conflict—or at least enable colleagues to have a more civil debate. Lincoln also used stories and humorous anecdotes to make a salient point (often indirectly), to minimize embarrassment, or to encourage further thinking by those within earshot of his remarks. As noted in Chapter 2, Lincoln was a legendary storyteller, and he also knew that many of the stories credited to him were not of his creation (much like today's aphorisms credited to Yogi Berra, such as "When you see the fork in the road, take it!"). Lincoln even made light of the famous remark inaccurately attributed to him about finding out the brand of whiskey Grant preferred and sending a bottle to the other generals. Lincoln simply indicated that attributing the remark to him added credibility to the story (Burlingame, 2008, Vol. 2, p. 517).

Phillips (1992) shares a wonderful anecdote Lincoln told about the hypocrisy of individuals who behave inappropriately and then criticize others for similar behavior. Lincoln's story is of the criminal who assaulted an innocent bystander:

> The criminal drew his revolver, but the assaulted party made a sudden spring and wrested the weapon from the hands of the would-be assassin. "Stop!" said the attacker. "Give me back that pistol; you have no right to my property." (p. 55)

An important point is that humor served a therapeutic function for Lincoln. Throughout his life, he suffered from bouts of depression, called "hypo" at that time (Shenk, 2005). The loss of a mother and a sister early in his life, the loss of two of his children, the harshness of frontier life, witnessing the cruelty of slavery, political defeats, and the Civil War could have destroyed any person. Humor was a lifeline for Lincoln. He once complained about a cabinet member who had little regard for light witticism, stating that "it required a surgical operation to get a joke into his head." When criticized by a congressman for telling a humorous story during a serious moment, Lincoln countered, "I say to you now, that were it not for this occasional *vent*, I should die" (Carwardine, 2006, p. 314).

A reason for the close bond between Lincoln and Secretary of State Seward was their mutual love of engaging conversation and a good joke. One evening during a dinner party at Seward's home, Lincoln's wit, humility, and frustration with the progress of the Army of the Potomac all converged when a guest complained about how difficult it was for him to secure a pass to visit Richmond, Virginia. Lincoln responded, "Well, I would be very happy to oblige you, if my passes were respected: but the fact is, sir, I have within the past two years, given passes to two hundred and fifty thousand men to go to Richmond, and not one has got there yet" (quoted in *Daily Morning Chronicle*, May 2, 1863, in Goodwin, 2005, p. 506).

As we reflect on Lincoln's character, based on the historical events, his words, stories, and wit, a portrait can be drawn that supports the idea that the whole is greater than the sum of its parts. Words without character are meaningless. Wilson (2006), in his exhaustive analysis of Lincoln's words, in the end looks to Aristotle to explain Lincoln's success:

> It is not true that the personal goodness revealed by the speaker contributes nothing to his power of persuasion; on the contrary, his character may almost be called the most effective means of persuasion he possesses. (*The Complete Works of Aristotle*, 1984, quoted in Wilson, 2006, p. 174)

Lincoln's Life and Work: Implications for School Leaders

This chapter addresses intangibles: personal example, character, loyalty, trust, humility, and humor. The power of these intangibles, which Lincoln so adeptly portrayed, has influenced leaders in profound ways throughout history. In fact, because of these characteristics, Lincoln's spirit has transcended time and still looms large in our conception of leadership. Seeking to explain this greatness, the foreword to *Time* magazine's bicentennial celebration issue on Lincoln succinctly states, "Abraham Lincoln is the archetypal American, because his extraordinary moral compass revolved around an ordinary life" (Knauer, 2009, p. vi). This observation reminds us that much of the school leader's work involves intangibles that others use to define that leader. These are often attributes that others "feel" or "perceive" and that influence opinions of the school leader and the assessment of whether that person's actions are characterized by integrity. If they are, respect and trust are earned. The qualities we often attribute to someone whose behavior is governed by a moral compass are "kindness, sensitivity, compassion, honesty, and empathy, [which] can also be impressive political resources" (Goodwin, 2005, p. xvii).

Personal example is a powerful tool for school leaders. Reflect upon what you do as a leader at the beginning of the day. Are you greeting students as they get off the bus? Handing out breakfasts and networking with staff and students? Where do people find you in the middle of the day? Are you walking through classrooms? What about the end of the day? Your behavior is observed and your example interpreted by organizational members—always. As University of Wisconsin Professor Kent Peterson reminds us, "What you pay attention to communicates what you value." Being self-aware about the messages conveyed by your behavior can actually be a tool for focusing the attention of organizational members. What you talk about in the hallways and on campus, for example, with students, staff, and parents, communicates volumes. One superintendent reflected, "I always try to greet people by name, or if I don't know the name, at least try to greet them with a warm 'hello' and 'how is your day going?' I talk about matters of teaching and learning. I mean to communicate, by example, that making a personal connection, coupled with an academic focus, will cause learning to soar. Hopefully, others will follow by example."

School principals must gain the trust of teachers, students, and parents. For example, during the teacher observation and conferencing phases, teachers need to believe that they can frankly discuss what is working in their classroom and take risks by trying out new strategies when teaching during observations to improve their practice. If teachers believe that principals will be overly critical of their performance, teachers are unlikely to go beyond their comfort level during a lesson, especially if they perceive that little margin for error exists.

Similarly, parents often wish to speak with the principal about a family situation, such as divorce or terminal illness, that may affect a student's behavior in the classroom. They want the principal to be understanding, respectful, and accessible. Both the observation process and the parent meeting will go much more smoothly, and be more effective, if trust exists. But what does trust entail? And why is it so critical?

After conducting a longitudinal study of Chicago school reforms involving 400 schools, Bryk and Schneider (2003) noted, "When school professionals trust one another and sense support from parents, they feel safe to experiment with new practices" (p. 41). Bryk and Schneider conclude that when "relational trust" is high, schools are more likely to make the changes that will help raise student achievement. The researchers found that four "vital signs" help to create the conditions that foster relational trust: respect, personal regard, competence, and integrity. In *The New Principal's Fieldbook* (Robbins & Alvy, 2004, p. 200), we describe these signs as follows:

1. *Respect.* Do staff members, parents, students, and community members acknowledge one another's dignity and ideas? Do organizational members treat one another in a courteous way during interactions?

2. *Personal Regard.* Do staff members and others in the larger school community care about one another personally and professionally? Are individuals willing to extend themselves beyond the formal requirements of the job or union contract?

3. *Competency in Core Role Responsibilities.* Do staff members, parents, and community members believe in one another's ability and willingness to fulfill role responsibilities effectively?

4. *Personal Integrity.* Can staff, parents, and school community members trust others to keep their word? Is there trust that the interests of children (their education and welfare) will be put first, even when tough decisions have to be made? (Based on the work of Bryk and Schneider.)

School leaders can look for evidence of these "vital signs" among staff and between principal and staff, as well as parents, as a guide for next steps. Bryk and Schneider (2003) conclude:

> Principals' actions play a key role in developing and sustaining relational trust. Principals establish both respect and personal regard when they acknowledge the vulnerabilities of others, actively listen to their concerns, and eschew arbitrary actions. Effective principals couple these behaviors with a compelling school vision and behavior that clearly seeks to advance the vision. This consistency between words and action affirms their personal integrity. Then, if the principal competently manages day-to-day school affairs, an overall ethos conducive to the formation of trust will emerge. (p. 43)

Three other attributes build and sustain trust over time: predictability, reliability, and reciprocity. When a leader's behavior is predictable, organizational members can count on a soothing consistency. For example, they know that walk-through visits are growth oriented and not evaluative—always. Reliability promotes trust because organizational members know they can count on the school leader to do as she says—to follow through. Finally, reciprocity builds trust because the leader vows to work just as hard in the leader's role as organizational members work in theirs.

Humility, another quality that engenders trust, is a characteristic of individuals who recognize that their triumphs rest upon the help and support of others. The premise, underscored by today's emphasis on professional learning communities, is that we cannot succeed in schools as isolated professionals. Reiterating this notion, a teacher leader reflected, "In our school, we believe that the interdependence among faculty members is the connective tissue that fuels our capacity to serve kids. We are always saying, 'Share the burden, give the credit' as a way of acknowledging the tremendous talent bank here that helps us amass the results that we do! Together we are better than alone."

Data teams in many schools mirror a sense of "team humility." That is, members of the team truly believe that the results they achieve are a function of the synergy that emerges as a consequence of their collaborative efforts. One strategy that school leaders can use to promote humility—besides modeling it themselves—is to encourage members of a professional learning community to engage in storytelling about individuals and teams within the school whose efforts make a difference in the achievements and ultimately the life paths of students.

Phillips (1992) addresses Lincoln's character by citing his behavior and what we know about successful business organizations and their leaders:

> The architecture of leadership, all the theories and guidelines, falls apart without honesty and integrity. It's the keystone that holds organizations together. Tom Peters reported in his research that the best, most aggressive, and successful organizations were the ones that stressed integrity and trust. 'Without doubt,' Peters stated, 'honesty has always been the best policy' . . . [and] James MacGregor Burns warned: 'Divorced from ethics, leadership is reduced to management and politics to mere technique.' (p. 52)

Speaking of dishonesty and lack of integrity, Phillips (1992) tells a story of how Lincoln compared a person "who smiled and then stabs you in the back to a tree that was being killed by a vine that covered its trunk: 'It's like certain habits of men,' said Lincoln. 'It decorates the ruin it makes'" (pp. 54–55).

Zenger and Folkman's (2002) research conclusions about the top 10 percent of leaders are based on data from more than 200,000 workers who rated more than 25,000 leaders. The researchers state:

> The conventional wisdom is that a lack of integrity or honesty is the classic fatal flaw. Indeed, we still believe that to be true. When people talk of the qualities they most admire, the most frequently noted characteristics are honesty, integrity, being a "straight shooter," saying what you really think, and never fudging the truth to please the group you are with. (pp. 159–160)

As school leaders reflect on the previous paragraph, they may identify leaders they have known who exemplified integrity and honesty in what they accomplished, and those who did not. In addition, Zenger and Folkman's leadership research and analysis demonstrates that a lack of emotional intelligence may be related to what they call "Five Fatal Flaws":

1. Inability to learn from mistakes.
2. Lack of core interpersonal skills and competencies.
3. Lack of openness to new or different ideas.
4. Lack of accountability.
5. Lack of initiative. (pp. 160–168)

Stories of Lincoln's life often illustrate that his ability to learn from mistakes, his interpersonal skills, his openness to new or different ideas, his dedication to study and reflection, and his sense of accountability and ambition, humbly stated, served him well. His example models the way for school leaders. Lincoln's well-documented use of language, anecdotes, and story invited audiences from all walks of life to engage with him. School leaders who are new to an organization have unique opportunities to connect with staff and the larger community through both deeds (aligning actions with words) and oral and written communication. The challenge, of course, is to select the words that humbly put one's ambitions—for example, developing a positive, collaborative, learning-focused school—in plain view of the constituents who will potentially benefit from that ambition.

Storytelling and anecdotes are a vivid way to emotionally connect and communicate with an audience. School leaders who have a "library" of such stories can pull out, at a moment's notice, a story or an anecdote that fits with the emotional tone of a situation. For instance, at the end of the school year, Harvey Alvy, then principal of the American Embassy School in New Delhi, was approached by a 1st grader who said, "Dr. Alvy, at the beginning of the year I didn't like you very much. But now, I like you better than my dog!" This story was shared with staff to lighten the moment of the year drawing to an end, but also to acknowledge the deep bonds that students had formed with teachers (and vice versa). It was shared as a tribute to the work that the staff had accomplished in making the school "a home for the heart and the mind." This story also reminds us about the role of instilling values in leadership actions and words.

As a public figure, Lincoln rarely missed an opportunity to share sacred national values such as the pursuit of liberty and the proposition that guaranteed equality to all. Phillips (1992) stresses that Lincoln embodied the values of the nation: "His integrity was, in short, the nation's integrity" (p. 53). This was illustrated clearly when Lincoln was traveling to Washington, D.C., in February 1861, to serve as the 16th president. Lincoln stopped at Independence Hall in Pennsylvania on February 22 and stated

> I am filled with deep emotion at finding myself standing here in the place where were collected together the wisdom, the patriotism, the devotion to principle, from which sprang the institutions under which we live. . . . All the political sentiments I entertain have been drawn, so far as I have been able to draw them, from the sentiments which originated, and were given to the world from this hall in which we stand. I have never had a feeling politically that did not spring from the sentiments embodied in the Declaration of Independence. . . . It was that which gave promise that in due time the weights should be lifted from the shoulders of all men, and that *all* should have an equal chance. (Basler, 1953–1955, Vol. IV, p. 240)

School leaders communicate similar values, "that *all* should have an equal chance," when in their own work and their work with others they commit themselves to closing the achievement gap and helping every student succeed.

Throughout the writings about Lincoln's life there is a well-documented use of humor. Humor releases endorphins, substances in the brain that produce feelings of well-being. Laughter, it has been said, puts people in a "limbic lock"—the closest distance between two brains. Daniel Goleman (1998), author of *Working with Emotional Intelligence*, writes as follows:

> We are all parts of each other's emotional tool kits, for better or worse; we continually prime others' emotional states, just as they do ours . . . our positive feelings about a company are to a large extent based on how the people that represent the organization make us feel. (p. 167)

These words emphasize the fact that still another tool in the school leader's toolbox is the skillful and strategic use of humor (as opposed to sarcasm). A well-timed joke or story that brings laughter can defuse a tense moment, infuse creativity, or refocus a team.

Reflecting on History and the Moment: Implications for the Future

We noted in Chapter 1 that defining leadership, especially great leadership, is a difficult task. However, there is almost universal agreement that success in carrying out the mission and vision of an endeavor—a cause—should be a primary gauge of leadership success. Based on leaders you admire, and your own ideas related to effective leadership, list the qualities and skills that you believe effective leaders possess. Use the space that follows to record two or three of your ideas.

- Effective leadership skills:

- Effective leadership qualities:

To make a statement about Lincoln's character, we began the introduction to this book with the following words from Frederick Douglass's 1876 speech at the dedication of the Freedmen's Monument in Washington, D.C.:

> Though high in position, the humblest could approach [Lincoln] and feel at home in his presence. Though deep, he was transparent; though strong, he was gentle; though decided and pronounced in his convictions, he was tolerant toward those who differed from him, and patient under reproaches. (Oakes, 2007, pp. 270–271)

As a school leader, after reading Douglass's words, consider how you might model the following traits:

- Accessibility:

- Transparency:

- Tolerance:

- Patience under reproaches:

- What else should you model?

Use this space to jot down any other ideas, insights, or new perspectives from this chapter that you wish to add to your repertoire as a school leader.

CHAPTER FIVE

Leading and Serving with Emotional Intelligence and Empathy

> He possessed extraordinary empathy—the gift or curse of putting himself in the place of another, to experience what they were feeling, to understand their motives or desires.
>
> —Doris Kearns Goodwin, *Team of Rivals*, p. 104

Goleman (1995) suggests that about 80 percent of adult success is based on emotional intelligence, which includes both personal and social competencies. The personal competencies relate to managing and understanding one's emotions; the social competencies relate to having empathy for individuals and groups and influencing and inspiring others (Goleman et al., 2002). In a study of effective principals in Ontario cited by Goleman (2006), the top principals "were empathetic, attentive, and understanding of others' feelings" (p. 79). Burlingame (2008), reflecting on Lincoln's greatness, stresses that Lincoln was void of a petty ego, which limits the effectiveness of many politicians; too often a politician's personal ambition eclipses the best interest of the people. Lincoln "managed to be strong-willed without being willful, righteous without being self-righteous, and moral without being moralistic" (Vol. 2, p. 833). White (2009) adds that following the embarrassing defeat of Union troops at Bull Run in July 1861, "as accusations swirled in Congress, the press, and the public, Lincoln refused to indulge in any finger pointing. If there would be any responsibility for defeat, he would bear it upon his broad shoulders" (p. 435). A person with a fragile ego would certainly have tried to pass the defeat on to others.

Lincoln's Own Story: A Path to Empathy

Ironically, Lincoln's personal suffering was likely an asset when it came to leading the nation. Because he had experienced the darkness that life sometimes offers up, such as poverty, and the loss of a parent and a sibling at an early age, there were few painful human emotions that he had not felt firsthand. Although Lincoln had attained modest wealth in his later years, as a child, an adolescent, and into his 20s, his life was very much working class, as he drifted from job to job, often carrying a substantial debt. He could relate to the common people because he had known that life. This is an important point for current school leaders, whether administrators or teachers. In their article "The Culturally Responsive Teacher," Villegas and Lucas (2007) stress that "to teach subject matter in meaningful ways and engage students in learning, *teachers need to know about their students' lives*" (p. 30, emphasis added). We cannot replace the emotional intelligence some adults may have because of background experiences that enable them to understand and connect with particular students or adults. Of course, all experiences can be meaningful; but we need to recognize the nature of our own experiences and what we can learn, or not learn, from them. However, if we do not have particular experiences, it is important to recognize our initial limitations and learn about cultural values and understandings to gain empathy, communicate better, and work effectively with colleagues and each student population. Emotional intelligence has clear implications related to cultural responsiveness.

Emotional Intelligence: A Vital Communication Tool

If emotional intelligence is a critical attribute for success among school leaders, from superintendents to principals to teacher leaders, it is fair to ask the following question: What does emotional intelligence look like? To answer this question, we can consider three documents written by President Lincoln: the Second Inaugural Address, delivered on March 4, 1865; the Temperance Address, delivered on February 22, 1842; and a letter sent to Fanny McCullough on December 23, 1862. Each document provides extraordinary insights into human nature, empathy, and the importance of hope.

The Second Inaugural Address

March 4, 1865, began as a rainy and windy morning. As President Lincoln stepped up to the podium to deliver his Second Inaugural Address, the sun fortuitously emerged from the clouds. The 30,000 attending the event knew that the Civil War was coming to a close. They expected to hear a speech of vindication, of triumph, a celebratory oration that would demonize the South (White, 2009). Instead they heard 701 visionary words concerning mutual responsibility, unification, and healing. Many historians consider the Second Inaugural Address to be Lincoln's greatest literary achievement. As you read the following sections from the speech, consider how Lincoln was demonstrating the qualities of an emotionally intelligent leader:

> At this second appearing to take the oath of the presidential office, there is less occasion for an extended address than there was at the first. . . . On the occasion corresponding to this four years ago, all thoughts were anxiously directed to an impending civil-war. All dreaded it—all sought to avert it. . . . Both parties deprecated war; but one of them would *make* war rather than let the nation survive; and the other would *accept* war rather than let it perish. And the war came. . . . One eighth of the whole population were colored slaves, not distributed generally over the Union, but localized in the Southern part of it. These slaves constituted a peculiar and powerful interest. All knew that this interest was, somehow, the cause of the war. . . . Each [side] looked for an easier triumph, and a result less fundamental and astounding. Both read the same Bible, and pray to the same God; and each invokes His aid against the other. It may seem strange that any men should dare to ask a just God's assistance in wringing their bread from the sweat of other men's faces; but let us judge not that we be not judged. The prayers of both could not be answered; that of neither has been answered fully. The Almighty has His own purposes. "Woe unto the world because of offences! for it must needs be that offences come; but woe to that man by whom the offence cometh!" If we shall suppose that American Slavery is one of those offences which, in the providence of God, must needs come, but which, having continued through his appointed time, He now wills to remove, and that He gives to both North and South, this terrible war, as the woe due to those by whom the offence came. . . . Fondly do we hope—fervently do we pray—that this mighty scourge of war may speedily pass away. Yet, if

God wills that it continue, until all the wealth piled by the bond-man's two hundred and fifty years of unrequited toil shall be sunk, and until every drop of blood drawn with the lash, shall be paid by another drawn with the sword, as was said three thousand years ago, so still it must be said "the judgments of the Lord, are true and righteous altogether."

With malice toward none; with charity for all; with firmness in the right, as God gives us to see the right, let us strive on to finish the work we are in; to bind up the nation's wounds; to care for him who shall have borne the battle, and for his widow, and his orphan—to do all which may achieve and cherish a just, and a lasting peace, among ourselves, and with all nations. (Basler, 1953–1955, Vol. VIII, pp. 332–333)

A sequential examination of Lincoln's address provides many insights. In the opening, he stresses that a long speech is unnecessary. There is no need to rehash detailed events of the past four years. Kindly, he states that both sides did not want war. This certainly surprised many in the crowd who wanted the president to censure, charge, and condemn the South. Lincoln was telling his audience: Do not expect this speech to be about singular Southern culpability for the war. The president then reminds the audience that initially his sole goal was to not let the nation perish. But his efforts failed. And then, in a simple but heartfelt four-word sentence, the president summarizes the tragic events of the past four years: "And the war came."

In the next section, Lincoln directly states that slavery was the cause of the war. Interestingly, when studying the Civil War in school today, we all review the "causes" of the war. In the Second Inaugural Address, Lincoln is telling the audience to be honest: "All knew that this interest was, somehow, the cause of the war." Then, the president takes a very risky yet candid step by implying that the righteousness of both sides is questionable. When Lincoln states, "Both read the same Bible," he is cautioning the audience about assuming that the North is free of sin. Here again, the humility of the president shows itself; he believes that "the Almighty has His own purposes," and Lincoln is not about to question that purpose. In fact, when moving from spiritual to worldly events, Lincoln talks of "American slavery," thereby not laying the blame solely on the South. "By saying 'American Slavery' Lincoln again uses inclusive language to assert that North and South must together own the offense" (White, 2009, p. 665). Because of 250 years of suffering that black Americans have been forced to bear, the Civil War is a mutual punishment that both sides must endure. Lincoln had great respect for the nation's founders, but he believed that the unresolved slavery issue was the nation's original sin. Joseph Ellis (2007), in his book *American Creation*, states, "The darkest shadow [on the founders] is unquestionably slavery, the failure to end it or at least to adopt a gradual emancipation scheme that put it on the road to extinction" (p. 10).

The last section of the Second Inaugural Address includes Lincoln's final surprise. Looking toward the future, he wants the audience to understand that healing can begin only with forgiveness and that a "just and lasting peace" could not occur unless all Americans were able "to bind up the nation's wounds." When we consider emotional intelligence as an abstract concept, "with malice toward none" makes sense. But as humans, are we capable of the kind of forgiveness that Lincoln asked for? John Wilkes Booth attended the second inaugural, and his crime a few weeks later greatly complicated attainment of the goals and hope that Lincoln sought. There simply was not another figure with Lincoln's influence to carry out the vision.

But forgiveness (not forgetting), empathy, and hope are crucial to reconcile former enemies. Remaining angry and vindictive limits one's ability to act thoughtfully and to develop respect for others. Perhaps the best modern example of an emotionally intelligent leader is Nelson Mandela. When he emerged from decades of brutal work, torture, and humiliation at Robben Island Prison off the coast of South Africa, his goal was reconciliation for all South Africans, not vengeance. He could not have become president of his nation without hope and a desire to address the needs of all South Africans.

The Temperance Address

When Lincoln made his speech to the Springfield Washington Temperance Society on February 22, 1842 (Washington's birthday), he was 33, a practicing Springfield lawyer, serving his fourth term in the state legislature, and still five years away from serving his one term in Congress. He enjoyed opportunities to speak and practice his skills, so he likely appreciated this chance to share his views on a crucial issue of the day—the reforming work of temperance societies that opposed alcohol use and "drunkards" (a common term of the 1840s).

In terms of emotional intelligence skills, Lincoln used the speech to build a relationship with members of his audience who may have suffered from alcohol abuse. Lincoln's speech did not portray the world as a battle between good and evil, in which he set himself apart from the world of drunkards (Miller, 2002). Although Lincoln was a nondrinker, he indicated that it was not because of any supreme authority or inner strength. Consider this excerpt from the speech:

> In my judgment, such of us as have never fallen victims, have been spared more from the absence of appetite, than from any mental or moral superiority over those who have. (Basler, 1953–1955, Vol. I, p. 278)

He also stressed that the traditional way of shunning excessive drinkers was ineffective because it would isolate victims and cause them to retreat from help. To help, one must forge relationships with the "head and heart." Using the lens of emotional intelligence, consider this excerpt:

> When the conduct of men [those who indulge in excessive drinking] is designed to be influenced, *persuasion*, kind, unassuming persuasion, should ever be adopted. It is an old and a true maxim, that a "drop of honey catches more flies than a gallon of gall [anger]." So with men. If you would win a man to your cause, *first* convince him that you are his sincere friend. Therein is a drop of honey that catches his heart, which, say what he will, is the great high road to his reason. (Basler, 1953–1955, Vol. I, p. 273, emphasis in original)

In this excerpt it is fascinating that Lincoln is suggesting that meaning is created through an emotional connection, based on relationships. The modern adage "People don't care what you know until they know that you care" certainly applies to Lincoln's thinking. Once the relational and emotional links are solid, then trust opens the door for the rational argument to stop drinking. In contrast, the next section of Lincoln's speech addresses the method used by "old reformers" of the temperance movement (what today we would refer to as a "deficit model"):

> On the contrary, assume to dictate to his judgment, or to command his action, or to mark him as one to be shunned or despised, and he will retreat within himself, [and] close all the avenues to his head and his heart. (Basler, 1953–1955, Vol. I, p. 273)

Although the full temperance address is quite lengthy (Lincoln's cogent and succinct writing style was still developing in 1842), the document again reveals his empathy with an audience. He considered it superficial to simply tell the drinker "you are to be pitied," "just restrain yourself," and "take the moral road." Before progress could occur, Lincoln believed that a bond must be established based on mutual respect and an understanding of the challenges that life sometimes presents to each of us.

Letter to Fanny McCullough

The third document that provides insight into President Lincoln's emotional intelligence skills is a letter that he wrote on December 23, 1862, to Fanny McCullough, the distraught daughter of Lieutenant Colonel William McCullough, who had been killed in Mississippi. Lincoln knew McCullough as a sheriff and a circuit court clerk in Bloomington, Illinois (Burlingame, 2008, Vol. 2, p. 462). The letter is particularly poignant because it is so personal. Lincoln is extremely candid; he understands Fanny's suffering ("I have had experience enough to know what I say"). The death of Lincoln's mother when he was 9 seems to be the obvious connection; however, when the president wrote this letter he was still suffering from the untimely death of his beloved son Willie, who had passed away in the White House only 10 months earlier. Lincoln wrote:

> Dear Fanny,
>
> It is with deep grief that I learn of the death of your kind and brave Father; and, especially, that it is affecting your young heart beyond what

is common in such cases. In this sad world of ours, sorrow comes to all; and, to the young, it comes with bitterest agony, because it takes them unawares. The older have learned to ever expect it. I am anxious to afford some alleviation of your present distress. Perfect relief is not possible, except with time. You can not now realize that you will ever feel better. Is not this so? And yet it is a mistake. You are sure to be happy again. To know this, which is certainly true, will make you some less miserable now. I have had experience enough to know what I say; and you need only to believe it, to feel better at once. The memory of your dear Father, instead of an agony, will yet be a sad sweet feeling in your heart, of a purer, and holier sort than you have known before. Please present my kind regards to your afflicted mother.

Your sincere friend   A. Lincoln
(Basler, 1953–1955, Vol. VI, pp. 16–17)

Although suffering is a primary theme, the letter also raises hope: "You are sure to be happy again." This must have been part of Lincoln's core belief, as his life was a constant struggle between setbacks and achievements. He understands Fanny's suffering, but he knows that the shroud of darkness will be lifted. Lincoln is a survivor, and he is pleading with Fanny to have the patience to live beyond the suffering. In addition, Lincoln's honest admission of his own suffering tells the reader that he is vulnerable, he is not invincible, but he must persevere. (Because perseverance and resilience are such salient qualities of Lincoln's character, we examine those topics in detail as a separate issue in Chapter 7.)

Demonstrating Restraint

One other point related to emotional intelligence needs to be addressed. At times, when Lincoln was angry or disappointed with someone's action, he would express his feelings by writing a heated letter—and then not send it. The famous Civil War historian Shelby Foote maintained that "Lincoln was his own psychiatrist" (Griessman, 1997, p. 41). To illustrate, Lincoln was very disappointed with General Meade after the Battle of Gettysburg because

Lincoln believed that Meade could have crippled Lee's army if he had pursued Lee following the battle. Strategically, Lincoln believed that the war was not so much about gaining territory as it was about destroying the enemy's army. Lincoln was disappointed, but he did not impulsively send an angry missive to Meade. The man who knew Lincoln best, his longtime Springfield law partner, Billy Herndon, understood this quality in "Mr. Lincoln." As Herndon (1889/1970) stated, "[Mr. Lincoln] seemed invariably to reflect and deliberate, and never acted from impulse so far as to force a wrong conclusion on a subject at any moment" (p. 37). So Lincoln wrote a letter to Meade, but his deliberate nature compelled him to withhold it. The letter that was never sent closed with the following thoughts:

> Again, my dear general, I do not believe you appreciate the magnitude of the misfortune involved in Lee's escape. He was within your easy grasp, and to have closed upon him would, in connection with our other late successes, have ended the war. . . . Your golden opportunity is gone, and I am distressed immeasurably because of it. [The footnote to the Meade letter in the *Collected Works* states, "The envelope containing this letter bears Lincoln's endorsement 'To Gen. Meade, never sent, or signed.'"] (Basler, 1953–1955, Vol. VI, p. 328)

Emotionally intelligent leaders understand that power has limits. "The irony is that the more power one accumulates, the less it should be used. Viewed another way, by exerting your power, you are taking away the powers of others" (George, 2007, p. 195). Emotionally intelligent leaders know, too, that arrogance, and the short-term benefits of a threat, cannot move a people in their souls. To win the Civil War, to retain the Union, and to end slavery demanded moving souls. To move souls a people must feel inspired. Lincoln provided that inspiration.

Lincoln's Life and Work: Implications for School Leaders

In this chapter we have explored Lincoln's proclivity to move people emotionally. Lincoln led others by the example of both his behavior and his writings.

His capacity in this regard was fueled by a keen knowledge of self, which enabled, through extrapolation, a deep and sensitive understanding of what others were feeling.

The work of school leaders usually has an emotional dimension as well. School principals and teacher leaders often play the roles of counselor, healer, priest, pastor, rabbi, imam, motivator, sage, or sounding board. Each of these functions is accompanied by complex emotional demands, and these demands often present themselves simultaneously. For instance, a reckless driving accident results in the death of a student. School leaders spring into action and find themselves doing grief counseling for parents, staff, and students; healing, by planning a way to memorialize the student; and coordinating with local law enforcement personnel to present an assembly on safe driving later in the year, and on a recurring basis.

Interestingly, these roles have little to do with the formal coursework in which leaders engage when they are preparing for careers in education. True, crisis management is part of the graduate curriculum in educational administration, but each crisis is different; the emotional grief present during a crisis—and the emotional intelligence needed to manage a crisis—can never be replicated in a university classroom. In fact, Daniel Goleman (1998) notes, "When IQ test scores are correlated with how well people perform in their careers, the highest estimate of how much difference IQ accounts for is 25 percent" (p. 19). Goleman adds, "The value of emotional intelligence for success grows more powerful the higher the intelligence barriers for entry into a field . . . 'soft skills' matter even more for success in 'hard fields'!" (pp. 19–20).

This notion was mirrored by Burt Swersey (in Goleman, 1998), who conducted a learning lab at the Rensselaer Polytechnic Institute on "The Five Secrets." Swersey told his engineering students that the five secrets of success were rapport, empathy, persuasion, cooperation, and consensus building. But instead of the lesson ending with the identification of the five secrets, Swersey had the students experience the five secrets by practicing them. The results were remarkable. "These sections turned out to be the best teams I've ever had in years of teaching 'Introduction to Engineering Design,'" said Swersey. "They not only worked better together than any students I've had, but they produced extremely ambitious innovative devices. I attribute a good part of their success to the time spent working on the five secrets" (Goleman, 1998, p. 230).

In organizations such as schools that rely on teamwork to get the job done, this learning lab provides a powerful lesson. That is, a focus on how members relate to one another is just as important as the product of team-work! Parker Palmer (2008) reiterates this point when he states the following:

> The external variables that we obsess over may be less important than we think. Not that we shouldn't attend to external aspects like money; of course, we should. But when we fail to attend to what goes on within and between people, we're making a huge mistake, a mistake sanctioned by the culture that keeps insisting that we look "out there" for solutions. (p. 14)

Just as Lincoln used his inner resources—self-understanding, empathy, the ability to manage his anger, the capacity to motivate himself when the outlook was bleak, and the ability to handle relationships—to communicate with, work with, and move the masses, so school leaders must rely on internal resourcefulness as well as technical skills in their work. Many do this intuitively. For those who do not, a quick review of what we know as the "Five Domains of Emotional Intelligence" may be helpful. (We have adapted the following section from *The New Principal's Fieldbook*, Robbins & Alvy, 2004, pp. 185–186.)

The five domains are "self-awareness, self-regulation, motivation, empathy, and social skills" (Goleman, 1998, November–December). *Self-awareness* involves the ability to put feelings into words, the ability to recognize and understand one's moods and emotions, and the skills to change one's moods to more positive ones. Self-aware individuals possess an accurate assessment of their strengths and weaknesses and often express self-deprecating humor. Competency in this domain also reflects an understanding of personality style and the effect of one's style on others, as well as specific strengths in multiple intelligences.

Self-regulation involves the skill of being able to manage emotions, including the ability "to control or redirect disruptive impulses and moods and the propensity to suspend judgment—to think before acting. [Lincoln modeled this by writing letters to those with whom he was angry and not sending them.] The hallmarks of this domain include trustworthiness and integrity, comfort with ambiguity and openness to change" (Goleman, 1998, November–December, pp. 92–102).

Motivation is the third domain of emotional intelligence. It involves the ability to delay gratification and the propensity to set goals and pursue them with zeal and perseverance. Researchers have found that the ability to motivate oneself even in the face of great difficulty is closely related to the spirit of optimism. Leaders who demonstrate this competency have high expectations for themselves, possess a strong drive for accomplishment even when confronted with failure, and "keep score" of their achievements.

Empathy is perhaps the most familiar of the five domains. We are all familiar with the saying "Walk a mile in your neighbor's shoes." This competency enables one to understand the emotions of others and provides the skills to interact with others responsively, according to their emotions. This capacity reflects a valuing of diversity and cross-cultural sensitivity. Expertise in this area usually enables people to build community, retain talent, and deliver quality customer care. These skills influence school climate, which in turn influences productivity. It has been said that "overall, the climate—how people feel about working at a company—can account for 20 to 30 percent of business performance" (Goleman et al., 2002, pp. 17–18).

The fifth domain of emotional intelligence is known as *social skills*. It involves what some call interpersonal polish—the unique ability to read another person's verbal or nonverbal cues and respond appropriately. Individuals who show competence in this area easily create rapport with others and are skilled in networking. Expertise in this area lends itself to team building and the ability to lead change.

As you read about these five domains, did you consider the domains in which Lincoln excelled, and the domains in which he may have been deficient? What about your own emotional intelligence? The next section provides you with the opportunity to reflect upon how Lincoln's words and deeds and the research on "soft skills" and emotional intelligence might influence your leadership work.

Reflecting on History and the Moment:
Implications for the Future

In *The Leadership Challenge*, Kouzes and Posner (2002) state:

> In assessing the believability of sources of communication—whether newscasters, salespeople, physicians, or priests; whether business managers, military officers, politicians, or civic leaders—researchers typically evaluate people on three criteria: their perceived trustworthiness, their expertise, and their dynamism. Those who are rated more highly on these dimensions are considered to be more credible sources of information. (p. 32)

Reflect on how you communicate with your constituents. Use the following table to analyze your actions and words using the three criteria noted by Kouzes and Posner.

Communicating with Constituents	
Criteria	Self-Assessment
Perceived trustworthiness	
Expertise	
Dynamism	

Identify any changes that you may wish to make in how you communicate with constituents.

Examine your strengths in each of the following five domains of emotional intelligence. Use this table to consider areas of strengths and how you display each of these domains in your work.

The Five Domains: Assessing Strengths		
Domain	**Current Assessment**	**How I Model This**
Self-Awareness		
Self-Regulation		
Motivation		
Empathy		
Social Skills		

Identify areas within the domains of emotional intelligence that you wish to strengthen.

Reread Lincoln's letter to Fanny, the young lady who lost her father. Consider which of the domains of emotional intelligence were modeled in this communication and write your thoughts here:

Use this space to jot down any other ideas, insights, or new perspectives from this chapter that you wish to add to your repertoire as a school leader.

CHAPTER SIX

Exercising Situational Competence and Responding Appropriately to Implement Effective Change

[Lincoln's] goals kept expanding as he tested how far he might go in his attempt to change history.

—Richard Striner, *Father Abraham: Lincoln's Relentless Struggle to End Slavery*, p. 3

When Abraham Lincoln took the presidential oath on March 4, 1861, seven Southern states had already seceded from the Union, and Jefferson Davis had been inaugurated as the provisional president of the Confederate States of America. Lincoln, a native of the border state of Kentucky, thought he understood the Southern position. However, events suggest that Lincoln had misjudged the depth and fervor of the Southern states' determination to follow through on their threat to secede and go to war (Fehrenbacher, 2009). Within seven weeks of the inaugural, Fort Sumter would fall, "and the war came."

Change is always complex and unpredictable. In the case of the United States Civil War, misjudgments, unyielding positions, chance, and destiny led to tragedy of a proportion no one could have predicted. The outcome of the war, however, ensured the preservation of a democratic Union and the end of slavery as an American institution. President Lincoln, of course, was responsible for significantly influencing events that would lead to this outcome. Examining his decisions, and how he influenced change, can provide constructive lessons for those serving in leadership positions. Winik (2001), in his analysis of Lincoln's sound decisions at the end of the war, states, "As every historian well knows, in the end it is not brilliance but judgment that separates the great leaders from the routine" (p. 241).

Cautious Expansion of the National Vision and Mission

At the time of his inauguration, Abraham Lincoln was inflexible on only two points related to the South. First, no state had the right to break up the Union. Second, he was opposed to the expansion of slavery. Despite his life-long opposition to slavery, the emancipation of the slaves in the Southern states was not yet within his presidential vision. Consider these excerpts from his First Inaugural Address:

> I have no purpose, directly or indirectly, to interfere with the institution of slavery in the States where it now exists. . . .

> I hold, that in contemplation of universal law, and of the Constitution, the Union of these States is perpetual. . . . It follows from these views that no State, upon its own mere motion, can lawfully get out of the Union. . . . Plainly, the central idea of secession, is the essence of anarchy. . . .

> One section of our country believes slavery is right, and ought to be extended, while the other believes it is wrong, and ought not to be extended. This is the only substantial dispute. (Basler, 1953–1955, Vol. IV, pp. 263–269)

Lincoln tempered the address to appeal to the Southern states and to Northern politicians who believed his earlier drafts were too provocative. There was a need to restrain the calls for war in both the North and the South. The famous closing section, "We are not enemies but friends" (examined in Chapter 2), was specifically written as a conciliatory gesture.

Initially, in his official capacity as president, Lincoln was unwilling to move on the issue of disturbing slavery in the South regardless of his personal views—he thought the Southern right to maintain slavery was a constitutional mandate. "For the first year and a half of the war, Lincoln's public rhetoric showed him acting with fidelity . . . especially [in relation to] . . .

the Declaration of Independence and the Constitution" (White, 2009, pp. 522–523). However, the length and catastrophic events of the war; the bloodshed; and a continual dialogue with friends, congressmen, and abolitionists eventually led to a profound change in Lincoln's thinking and the future direction of the nation. Sinha (2008) notes that "emancipation was a complex process that involved the actions of the slaves, the Union army, Congress and the president" and that we often overlook "the largely forgotten role that [black and white] abolitionists played in influencing the president's evolving view on slavery and race during the Civil War" (p. 168). On January 1, 1863, the Emancipation Proclamation was authorized as an executive military act (which included permission to recruit African American soldiers). By the fall of 1864, Lincoln was running on an election platform that favored the "unconditional surrender" of the insurrectionist states and a Thirteenth Amendment to the Constitution abolishing slavery in the United States (McPherson, 2008b). The aims of the war and the course of history had changed.

The Emancipation Proclamation was criticized when issued—and is criticized today—as a document that was too conservative because it did not immediately free the slaves and it affirmed slavery in areas that were not part of the insurrection. In reality, based on the results of the war, the proclamation heralded the end of slavery and changed the war from a conflict about preserving the Union and its democratic principles to a moral crusade to abolish slavery and, in effect, expand the democratic principles of the nation's founders.

Situational Awareness, Timing, and Change

Lincoln knew the importance of timing. Many believed Lincoln had acted too slowly. But those who knew Lincoln, including Billy Herndon, Stephen Douglas, and Frederick Douglass, learned that although he may have been slow to move, once he did so, going forward meant not looking back. Consider Lincoln's letter to Horace Greeley during the summer of 1862, reviewed in Chapter 2 ("My paramount objective in this struggle is to *save* the Union"). Although Lincoln had already decided to issue the Emancipation

Proclamation, he did not share that news with Greeley. In Lincoln's view, public opinion was not ready for the document; thus he followed Secretary of State Seward's advice to wait for a military victory. Douglas Wilson's (2006) analysis of Lincoln's response to the Greeley letter is significant:

> Indeed, what this episode suggests in retrospect is that one of the things Lincoln was most criticized for by members of his own party—his slowness to act—was in reality a superior sense of timing. But the publication of the Greeley letter was the unveiling of what would prove to be an even greater asset, his ability to shape public opinion with his pen. (pp. 160–161)

Lincoln's decision to respond to Greeley was itself a novel idea. Previously, presidents had not used the bully pulpit to engage in a dialogue with newspaper editors. Some thought that it was demeaning for a president to engage in this type of dialogue. Most, however, agreed that using newspapers in this way was a masterstroke by the president to influence public opinion (Burlingame, 2008).

As we reflect on Lincoln's timing and issuing of the proclamation, we must also consider this question: How could a man with such a reverence for the nation's founders and firm belief in the sacredness of the original Constitution be willing to change his position and step outside of his comfort zone? A simple answer would be that the war was going poorly and Lincoln had to change his strategy. But Lincoln would not have made a strategic change if the change compromised his vision of a democratic Union. In his analysis of change, Evans (1996) insightfully suggests that "people must first be sufficiently dissatisfied with the present state of affairs—and their role in maintaining it—or they have no reason to endure the losses and challenges of change" (p. 57). Lincoln saw the stark reality during the summer of 1862: the state of affairs may have led to the end of the war, but without the president's goals being met. Situational competence demanded a change that would not only preserve the Union but also raise the moral stakes of the effort. Profound change was necessary.

To understand Lincoln's change of thinking, one must review a closing section of his annual message to Congress sent on December 1, 1862. Today we call this message the State of the Union Address. As you read this section, consider what Lincoln is saying about the change process:

> We can succeed only by concert [agreement]. It is not "can *any* of us *imagine* better?" but "can we *all* do better?" . . . The dogmas of the quiet past, are inadequate to the stormy present. The occasion is piled high with difficulty, and we must rise with the occasion. As our case is new, so we must think anew, and act anew. We must disenthrall our selves, and then we shall save our country. (Basler, 1953–1955, Vol. V, p. 537, emphasis in original)

This message, delivered on the eve of the Emancipation Proclamation, is critical in helping us to understand what Lincoln must have been thinking. "Dogmas" are core beliefs, and he is stating that the core beliefs of the past will not help save the nation. To rise to the occasion, "we must think anew." The context has changed; thus new ideas and innovative strategies will have to be created to address the new context. These new strategies, based on freeing an oppressed people, eventually destroyed the South's capacity to use slave labor to support its war effort and, as noted earlier, resulted in the recruitment of African American soldiers. The courageous performance of these soldiers during the war not only affected events on the ground but also became an important public relations weapon in the hands of the president.

Additionally, thinking and acting anew meant using a military strategy that most Union generals had opposed during the early stages of the war. As the war progressed, Lincoln believed it was important to fight a war of total conquest, not just for territorial concessions. In *Supreme Command: Soldiers, Statesmen, and Leadership in Wartime*, Cohen (2002) stresses the following:

> Lincoln's insistence on turning the Army of the Potomac against Lee's army rather than against the enemy's capital is evidence of [an appreciation of the strategic conditions], as was his understanding—far earlier than most of his generals—that the war would become a revolutionary struggle which would require the shattering of the South's will to resist, not merely the defeat of its forces in the field. (p. 213)

"In all five functions as commander in chief—policy, national strategy, military strategy, operations, and tactics—Lincoln's conception and performance were dynamic rather than static" (McPherson, 2008a, p. 267). The dynamic strategy, according to McPherson, occurred *after* Lincoln gave up his effort to restore the Union with slavery contained in the border states and the South. That effort did not cripple the South enough to end the war—in fact, that effort failed. The national military strategy changed when Lincoln embraced the abolition of slavery as part of a military effort to destroy the Confederacy.

Thinking and Acting Anew: Implementing Revolutionary Change

To gain a greater understanding of what Lincoln was trying to accomplish and how his views changed, it is helpful to consider Heifetz and Linsky's (2002) explanation of technical and adaptive challenges, and Evans's (1996) description of first-order and second-order change. The "technical challenges" Heifetz and Linsky are referring to involve the implementation of change efforts based on problems we have faced before and solutions in which we "have the necessary know-how and procedures" (p. 13). Adaptive challenges, on the other hand, "require experiments, new discoveries, and adjustments" (p. 13), not just from the leader but also from a host of individuals. Thinking in new ways must occur and must include "changing attitudes, values, and behaviors" (p. 13). Heifetz and Linsky stress that with adaptive change, internalization of the problem must occur; that is, personal commitment to make the change is critical. Moreover, "the single most common source of leadership failure we've been able to identify . . . is that people, especially those in positions of authority, treat adaptive challenges like technical problems" (p. 14).

Evans (1996), citing the seminal 1974 work of Watzlawick, Weakland, and Fisch, notes that first-order change efforts strive "to improve the efficiency or effectiveness of what we are already doing" (p. 5). Second-order changes create a new world view "and modify the very way an organization is put together, altering its assumptions, goals, structures, roles and norms . . . [and require changing] beliefs and perceptions" (p. 5).

Consider Lincoln's statement "As our case is new, so we must think anew, and act anew." In the Heifetz and Linsky (technical and adaptive) and Evans (first- and second-order) models of change, a critical concept includes changing fundamental ways of thinking: our assumptions, norms, structures, values, attitude, and, eventually, behaviors. In today's language we might say that adaptive and second-order change is necessary when, to use Lincoln's phrase, "the occasion is piled high with difficulty." Interestingly, Heifetz and Linsky note that the reality of September 11, 2001, meant the U.S. government would have to address terrorism with the tools of adaptive change, not technical change. They stress, however, that the use of the tools of technical change should not be diminished: "What makes a problem technical is not that it is trivial; but simply that its solution already lies within the organization's repertoire" (p. 18).

This point is paramount when considering the Lincoln example and how he responded to the contextual events of the American Civil War. At first he thought he was dealing with technical challenges. To illustrate, Lincoln believed, following his election, that by remaining firm on opposing both secession and the expansion of slavery, he had a good chance of avoiding war. He conceded other points and believed that compromise might work. During the war he tried what appeared to him to be "moderate" tactics and endorsed schemes such as compensating states for freeing slaves and encouraging the colonization of former slaves to Africa, Haiti, or Central America. These were not solutions to an adaptive challenge.

All of his life, Lincoln favored a moderate approach to most issues. In Illinois in the 1850s, his opposition to the expansion of slavery was as close to an extreme position as any he had taken since questioning, during his congressional term, the Polk administration's justification for initiating the Mexican War. Abolition and the language of abolitionists always seemed extreme to him. In fact, during the Lincoln-Douglas debates of 1858, Stephen Douglas tried to portray Lincoln as a "Black Republican," an extremist on slavery and on the rights of African Americans (Oakes, 2008). To fight the accusations, appear moderate, and gain political support from those watching the debate, Lincoln parried Douglas's ideas with arguments that swayed the crowd but, at times, were racist in tone. We are reminded that Lincoln had his shortcomings.

We will never know the exact moment when Lincoln realized that his moderate approach to winning the war and addressing the slavery issue was unworkable. Based on his personality, it was unlikely that Lincoln experienced an "aha!" moment. "By temperament Lincoln favored careful reflection, not impulsive action" (Carwardine, 2006, p. 28). And, although he was not using the language of adaptive or second-order change, his December 1 message to Congress revealed that he certainly knew the risks of a profound shift.

Based on President Lincoln's successful actions during the Civil War, we can draw some conclusions on how he managed change:

- He never wavered on the initial mission to preserve the Union, maintain its democratic institutions, and defend against the expansion of slavery.
- When he expanded the mission to include the emancipation of slaves, he maintained that the action strengthened the Union and would, in fact, strengthen the democratic institutions.
- He faced the brutal facts when events on the ground were weakening his ability to accomplish the mission.
- He recognized that the state of affairs required new thinking—old models of compromise were unworkable.
- His flexibility and willingness to listen to voices on all sides of a debate enabled him to gain the knowledge necessary to act effectively.
- He recognized the importance of public opinion and welcomed the "dialogue" created by newsprint. (He did not live in a bubble isolated from the public.)
- He recognized the power of timing.
- He learned from mistakes.
- He was firm, yet flexible.

As Lincoln prepared his remarks for Gettysburg, in November 1863, the war was beginning to slowly shift in favor of the Union. As his train moved from Washington to Pennsylvania, did he consider how much his views had changed since November of 1860? The nation, post–Civil War, was going to be a very different place from the one he grew up in, and he had influenced how it was going to be different. Lincoln must have felt some satisfaction in knowing that the democratic ideals established by the founding generation had taken another step forward because of his actions. The work was still unfinished, but his words at Gettysburg on November 19, 1863, humbly acknowledged that the nation had made progress:

> It is for us the living, rather, to be dedicated here to the unfinished work which they who fought here have thus far so nobly advanced. It is rather for us to be here dedicated to the great task remaining before us—that from these honored dead we take increased devotion to that cause for which they gave the last full measure of devotion—that we here highly resolve that these dead shall not have died in vain—that this nation, under God, shall have a new birth of freedom—and that government of the people, by the people, for the people, shall not perish from the earth. (Basler, 1953–1955, Vol. VII, p. 23)

Lincoln's Life and Work: Implications for School Leaders

In this chapter we have explored Lincoln's unwavering dedication to the democratic ideals of freedom, as well as his actions to realize that vision. But, as historical accounts of his positions attest, his writings, words, and behavior were tempered and changed by a powerful understanding of "situational awareness." Lincoln's astute sense of timing, his refusal to abandon his core values in the face of adversity, and his propensity for giving credit to those who furthered the democratic cause of freedom all contributed to his ultimate success. Lincoln's thoughts, articulated in his speeches, and his decisions that influenced action portray a deep understanding of the complexity of change. He also demonstrated a relentless commitment to invent new ways of envisioning or revisioning problems when familiar solution strategies, used in the past, failed to measure up to the current challenges. In all of Lincoln's words and deeds, what was never absent was a deep, sensitive, empathetic understanding of the human toll incurred as a result of any action. As Evans (1996) reminds us, "Although change usually represents loss, from such loss comes not only despair but also innovation. Indeed despair is often the root of innovation" (p. 59). Lincoln's example, once again, reminds us that when the war was going poorly for the Union, he made a strategic change, stepping out of his comfort zone and aligning his actions with a profound reverence for his vision of a democratic Union.

The accounts of how Lincoln exercised situational competence to facilitate change have profound implications for school leaders on many levels. First, school leaders frequently face "occasions piled high with difficulty." These often require both a technical and an emotional response. Second, school leaders work with both first-order change—merely tinkering with existing systems—and adaptive, second-order change, which requires a fundamental transformation of existing systems and processes with new ways of thinking, responding, and operating. It is important to be able to distinguish between the two. Third, change represents, by its very nature, a sense of loss—loss of the familiar. Fourth, change is context driven. What works in one culture, for instance, may fail miserably in another because of the unique characteristics of each context. Fifth, effective change agents possess specific competencies as human beings that distinguish them from their mediocre counterparts. In the paragraphs that follow, we explore each of these fundamental notions, informed by Lincoln's example, current research, and successful, contemporary practice.

School leaders' work is complex, challenging, and multidimensional. For example, a middle school principal, seeking to enhance safety for students, changed the pick-up location for buses and the flow of traffic. The principal was overwhelmed with dramatic, often furious responses from parents and students. She was puzzled by the volume of written and oral feedback she received as a consequence of what seemingly was a minor, technical change. But it was not "minor" to parents or students. "Who do you think you are?" wrote one parent. "Don't you know that it's always been the other way—even when I attended school here as a child? How dare you change this!"

Though the focus of the change, in this case, was firmly linked to student safety, progress, and development, its private meaning for stakeholders was quite different. It represented loss of the familiar. School leaders need to realize that when the "structure of meaning is rooted in feelings and experiences that have great emotional significance, . . . perceptions and purposes can rarely be altered by rational explanations alone" (Evans, 1996, p. 30). Yet, swept up with the urgency of a problem and the promise of a solution, school leaders often fail to realize that those who will have to adapt to a change may reel with agony as a consequence of its implementation. Recognizing that technical changes bring emotional reactions more often than not, school leaders can proactively plan for change by inviting individuals who will be affected by it to be part of naming the problem and engaging in the process to address it. Evans succinctly and insightfully describes the duality of change when he writes, "The different meanings change has for its advocates and its targets mirrors a fundamental division within each of us, between our overt embrace of change and our conservative impulse to resist it" (p. 38).

School leaders are now attempting reforms that are far more extensive and complex than ever before. Many of these fail because they neglect a fundamental consideration of the culture of the school—that is, the context into which the change will be introduced. Further, many reform efforts fail to distinguish between first- and second-order change.

As noted earlier, Evans, building on the landmark work of Watzlawick, Weakland, and Fisch (1974), reminds us that first-order change is simply directed at making minor changes in existing practice. Second-order change is systemic; it requires organizational members to change their beliefs and perceptions. An example of a second-order change that many school leaders have embraced is changing from a traditional schedule of seven, eight, or nine instructional periods to a block schedule with fewer daily periods made up of longer amounts of instructional time. In addition to planning for the type of change, taking into account cultural members' values, beliefs, and assumptions is instrumental in fashioning how the change is introduced and whether its implementation will be successful—or not. Michael Fullan once said at an ASCD conference, "The proof is in the 'putting.' How the change is put forth will, in large part, determine its success or failure." School leaders who pave the way for successful change often spend time talking to the informal power brokers in the workplace culture. They solicit their insights, ideas, and commitment so that the change takes root in fertile soil. Successful implementation of a change depends heavily upon whether the envisioned change has meaning for those who must implement it.

Schlechty (2001) reminds us that "compared to sustaining change, starting change is relatively easy" (p. 39). He points out that this is why more changes are initiated in schools than are sustained. In writing about the challenge of sustaining change, Schlechty notes, "Two things sustain change; one is a leader or leadership group that acts as a change agent; the other is a system or group of systems that supports change" (p. 40). This explains why, when the school culture does not have the capacity to sustain a change effort, "the change rarely outlasts the tenure of the change agent" (p. 40). A key leadership task, then, is to study and then create those conditions within the culture that will support and sustain a change. This is often a huge challenge because most cultures are structured to protect the status quo. Working with school leaders in Napa, California, Robert Garmston once explained a change formula as follows: "A vision of what might be, plus a dissatisfaction with what is, must be greater than the cost of a change." Douglas Reeves (2009), writing about how difficult change is to implement, states, "The fear of pain and death is not, for many people, greater than their unwillingness to change" (p. 1). Perhaps the reason individuals are prone to resist change is because, as noted earlier, it does represent loss of familiar ways of doing things and of the comfort of familiarity, and it adds the pressure of new demands looming over one's traditional role.

Kanter (1997) offers an additional bit of advice, reflecting about how, if a change doesn't produce immediate results, it's tempting to move on to the next new thing:

> The difference between success and failure is often just a matter of time: staying with the project long enough to overcome the unexpected developments, political problems, or fatigue that can come between a great-sounding plan and actual results. A basic truth of management—if not of life—is that nearly everything looks like failure in the middle. At the same time, the next project always looks more attractive (because it is all promise, fresh, and untried). (p. 129)

School leaders who understand this reality will more likely find the inner strength to persevere and reach to ensure that the organizational vision becomes reality.

Research and examples of successful practice offer commentary on characteristics of leaders who are successful change agents. Bennis (1984) notes, "It is the ability of the leader to reach the souls of others in a fashion which raises human consciousness, builds meaning, and inspires human intent that is the source of power" (p. 70). To reach the souls of others, school leaders must be skillful in perspective taking. They must understand the perspective of those affected by change and have empathy for them. They must be able to tell stories that touch constituents' souls. Jay Conger (1989) identifies four stages of charismatic leadership that can be transformational:

1. Being sensitive to constituents' needs, seeing current problems as opportunities, and building a vision that addresses them.
2. Articulating this vision in a way that simultaneously makes the status quo unacceptable and the new vision appealing.
3. Establishing trust among followers through proof of sincere commitment to the vision.
4. Showing the means to fulfill the vision, including the setting of their own personal example, the empowerment of others, and the use of unorthodox methods. (pp. 25–34)

We see, in this list, several attributes that reflect Lincoln's example: being sensitive to constituents' needs, vision building and articulating the vision, creating trust, modeling the way, and illustrating the steps to fulfilling the vision. School leaders who commit to addressing these four stages in their daily words and deeds will be able to move organizational members emotionally and, as a consequence, will have a greater chance of facilitating change in the organization.

Kouzes and Posner (1987) put it this way: "The true force that attracts others is the force of the heart" (p. 125). Trust is at the root of transformation. It is the critical link between the leader and organizational members. In school or district cultures where it is present, staff members are focused, energized, loyal, and productive. School leaders need to reflect upon how they might build, reinforce, and sustain high levels of trust among their constituents. Practitioners would advise "walking your talk, being consistent, fair, honest, genuine, showing respect for others, honoring diversity and diverse views" (a principal's voice). A teacher leader added to this list: "passionate about the organization and its mission, good communicator, acting in accordance with your personality, commonsense approach, understanding of self, and an accurate perception of how others see you."

Evans (1996) summarized research on principals who were successful change agents: "All fulfilled four key roles (resource provider, instructional resource, communicator, visible presence) but did so in very different ways" (p. 199). School leaders might assess their skills in these four areas. Self-knowledge—an understanding of one's strengths and weaknesses—and a commitment to continually learn and grow are hallmarks of successful leaders. These attributes serve as an anchor in the spinning world of change—a world in which change is a constant in a sociopolitical context. It occurs simultaneously at the individual and organizational levels, as well as both inside and outside individuals, leaders, and organizations.

Indeed, "the measure of a leader may well be his or her capacity to understand and successfully work with change—to stimulate it, shape it, nurture it, guide it, manage it, revise it, and keep the change journey going" (Robbins & Alvy, 2009, p. 69). Abraham Lincoln modeled the way.

Reflecting on History and the Moment: Implications for the Future

Think of a change effort that you will be facilitating or that you are currently immersed in. For each of the following points, use the space to jot down your thoughts or experiences.

For successful change and innovation to occur, school leaders must do the following:

- Support innovative, coherent, and meaningful ideas of substance.

- Understand the importance of building relationships and trust, and helping people develop.

- Thoroughly understand and navigate the change process.

The following list represents a synthesis of ideas from Michael Fullan's classic work, *The New Meaning of Educational Change* (2007):

- Organizations must create the capacity for change, shared meaning, and continuous improvement; the innovation is not the only goal.
- Sustained change involves "lateral capacity building," school-to-school sharing (p. 56).
- Successful leaders build teacher capacity, distribute leadership, and promote program coherence (i.e., specific learning goals, sustained over time).
- Leaders set direction with a moral compass, "develop" people, and create collaborative communities—a key to change is that relationships improve.
- Change includes three nonlinear phases: initiation, implementation, and institutionalization.
- Change is a journey in context; a process, not a destination.
- Resisters have some good ideas.
- Having a great passion for a change can get in the way if it means ignoring the ideas of others and the change process. Leaders need to be committed to the change process as well as the change.
- Sometimes charismatic gurus hurt the process if they cultivate disciples, rather than independent thinkers.

- "Today, no serious change effort would fail to emphasize the key role of the principal" (p. 156).

In summary: Change necessitates shared meaning and capacity building, focused on results, relationships, collaboration, and continuous improvement.

After reading through these important insights, reflect on and consider the implications for your work in facilitating change; use the space here to write down your thoughts.

Use this space to jot down any other ideas, insights, or new perspectives from this chapter that you wish to add to your repertoire as a school leader.

CHAPTER SEVEN

Rising Beyond Personal and Professional Trials Through Tenacity, Persistence, Resilience, and Courage

> The hope is not that suffering will go away, for with Lincoln it did not ever go away. The hope is that *suffering, plainly acknowledged and endured, can fit us for the surprising challenges that await.*
>
> —Joshua Wolf Shenk, *Lincoln's Melancholy,*
> p. 216, emphasis added

The test of leadership comes when difficult decisions need to be made that will profoundly change the ethos of a school, a business, or a nation. Sometimes those decisions are so dramatic—affecting habits, values, and core beliefs—that forces within the culture refuse to budge and, in fact, threaten the source of the change. "In the most extreme cases, some leaders like Anwar Sadat and Yitzhak Rabin have been assassinated because they challenged the norms and values of their communities" (Heifetz & Linsky, 2004, p. 34). Heifetz and Linsky use the phrase "leadership on the line" to refer to the vulnerable positions of leaders when they make courageous decisions to reach worthy goals that will, in addition, cause significant cultural discomfort.

Courage During the Storm: Dogged Tenacity

School leaders on every level also must make difficult decisions that will change the culture. Again, the Lincoln example is relevant. The resistance and criticism that he received for the difficult decisions made throughout the Civil War were overwhelming. But he persisted. Winik (2001) accurately states:

> Lincoln pressed on [despite the failure of several generals], weathering his own mistakes, and equally weathering the brittle highs and deepening lows of the war. If he can best be described during this period, it is with two words: dogged tenacity. Dogged tenacity. It is a simple explanation for greatness. But, in Lincoln's case, also probably quite true. (p. 245)

What inner character traits enabled Lincoln to remain so tenacious, sticking to his mission during the war years, especially with all of the criticism and resistance?

The scale of resistance that leaders face, even when making obvious and necessary decisions, will surprise both veterans and neophytes—especially when harsh criticism, sometimes from unexpected sources, is aimed directly at the leader. Leaders must find out what their individual capacity is to cope when difficult times occur, when the wounds are inflicted. Questions to ask include: Will I remain resilient? Will I have the courage to take the organization to the next level? Ackerman and Maslin-Ostrowski (2004) ask, "How does a reasonable, well-intentioned person, who happens to be a school leader, preserve a healthy sense of self in the face of a host of factors that may challenge that self or even lead to a wounding crisis?" (p. 28). The good news, they say, is that these challenging times offer the opportunity to learn "how leadership truly emerges from our inner struggles and how we consciously project that inner life onto others" (p. 28).

President Lincoln had to find a reservoir of strength to handle the unrelenting critics and to maintain his vision of the Union and emancipation during the Civil War. School leaders can learn much from his experience. Just consider the criticism he heard and read, as indicated in these examples:

- "A first-rate *second rate* man [with] no mind whatsoever."
- "He has no stiffness in him."
- "A rather slow intellect . . . he has no experience of men and events, and no knowledge of the past."

- "[Lincoln is a] prevaricating, irresolute, weak, besotted [president]."
- "The president is an idiot . . . the original gorilla . . . a well meaning baboon."
- "A third-rate country lawyer who once split rails and now splits the union." (Burlingame, 2008; Holzer, 2009; Phillips, 1992)

Strength from Experience

In Lincoln's case, the ability to face and rise to a challenge came from the personal narrative of his life. Lincoln knew the story of his past and recognized that he could shape the story of his future. Lincoln knew that he lacked the formal education to compete with the privileged. Self-education was his only option. Lincoln had the patience and tenacity to teach himself, to learn the craft of the surveyor, to learn the law, to work on his oratorical skills, and to improve his writing skills. Having only one year of formal schooling would not stop him from enjoying Shakespeare, Byron, or Robert Burns. He would become a lifelong learner. Those who encountered Lincoln would learn that although he may not have had the benefits of a privileged education, he should not be taken for granted. An Illinois law associate, Leonard Swett, cautioned, "Any man who took Lincoln for a simple-minded man . . . would very soon wake up with his back in a ditch" (Donald, 1995, p. 149).

Even before embarking on a legal career, Lincoln decided, at age 23, to run for the Illinois legislature from the district that included New Salem. He lost this early contest but impressed the local folks enough to receive 277 of 300 votes in the New Salem area. He may have lacked formal education and privilege, but his character impressed those who knew him best. When running for the legislature, his campaign message on March 9, 1832, closed with the following words:

> Every man is said to have his peculiar ambition. Whether it be true or not, I can say for one that I have no other so great as that of being truly esteemed of my fellow men, by rendering myself worthy of their esteem. *How far I shall succeed in gratifying this ambition is yet to be developed.* I am young and unknown to many of you. I was born and have ever remained

in the most humble walks of life. I have no wealthy or popular relations to recommend me. (Basler, 1953–1955, Vol. I, pp. 5–9, emphasis added)

Right from the start, Lincoln always accepted his origins, but he hoped to someday be "truly esteemed," to be respected. To earn that respect it was necessary to "render myself worthy." So the ambition was there, supported by a core value: do not reward me unless I earn it. Interestingly, his New Salem campaign message was telling the voters that his personal story was still unfolding: "How far I shall succeed in gratifying this ambition is yet to be developed." Two years later, a positive development occurred: he won the first of four successive victories for the state legislature.

Resilience: The Courage to Battle Back

According to those who knew him best, Lincoln's nature, his personality, was "tinged with sadness" (Joseph Gillespie in Holzer, 2009, p. 39). When his courtship with Mary Todd was going though a fragile period, his melancholy took hold. He told his law partner and friend John Stuart:

> I am now the most miserable man living. If what I feel were equally distributed to the whole human family, there would not be one cheerful face on the earth. Whether I shall ever be better I can not tell; I awfully forebode I shall not. To remain as I am is impossible; I must die or be better, it appears to me. (Basler, 1953–1955, Vol. I, p. 229)

Goodwin (2005) describes how Lincoln's resilience helped him recover. As his lifelong friend Joshua Speed recalled, Lincoln, then in his early 30s, was unwilling to surrender to his depressed state because, as Lincoln stated to Speed, he had "done nothing to make any human being remember that he had lived, and that to . . . link his name with something that would redound to the interest of his fellow man was what he desired to live for" (pp. 99–100). Goodwin closes this episode by stating that "resilience, conviction, and strength of will [helped] Lincoln gradually recover from his depression" (p. 100). Lincoln was driven to succeed; in the words of his longtime law partner Billy Herndon, "His ambition was a little engine that knew no rest" (Thomas, 1952, p. 153).

One cannot help but think of the Emancipation Proclamation when reflecting on Lincoln's origins and desire to "link his name with something that would redound to the interest of his fellow man." True, it took courage, tenacity, and persistence to move forward with the proclamation on January 1, 1863. But the document also ensured that Lincoln's name would endure. Lincoln must have been thinking about his humble origins and desire to make his mark when he stated to Secretary Seward as he was about to sign the proclamation, "I never, in my life, felt more certain that I was doing right, than I do in signing this paper" (Burlingame, 2008, Vol. 2, p. 469).

Lincoln had the ambition, and he wanted to make a difference. He wanted others to remember that he had lived. A career in politics could satisfy both his ambition and his desire to make a difference. Ironically, his political life may also provide us with a plausible explanation of how he managed to survive the melancholy periods. Lincoln enjoyed the give and take, the debate, the friendships, and the possibilities to make a difference that a political career offered. And he kept at it, serving in the Illinois state legislature, serving as a United States congressman, twice running for the Senate, and eventually, largely due to his senatorial campaign debates with Stephen Douglas in 1858, becoming president. Princeton scholar Sean Wilentz (2009) suggests that today's historians, captivated by Lincoln's literary and human relations skills, overlook his "political astuteness" (p. 26). Wilentz concludes, "[Lincoln] was never too good for politics. Quite the contrary: for him, politics—ordinary, grimy, unelevating politics—was itself a good, and an instrument for good" (p. 47). Miller (2002) adds, "If Abraham Lincoln was not a politician, then words have no meaning" (p. xv).

The Importance of Camaraderie

In addition to providing the opportunity to make a difference and to use his oratorical skills, politics offered Lincoln camaraderie. As noted earlier, the difficult decisions that leaders make place them "on the line" (Heifetz & Linsky, 2004). Leaders feel alone, with the weight of the world on their shoulders.

Consider Lincoln's words when he heard of the Union defeat at Chancellorsville in May of 1863: "My God! My God! What will the country say! What will the country say!" (White, 2009, p. 561). To survive during the difficult times, leaders need to network and to nurture allies, friends, and intimates they can count on. Although Lincoln had very few close friends throughout his life, his love of storytelling, jokes, and a laugh indicate that his resilience and ability to persist during difficult times were helped by the moments of lightheartedness. "What others derived from a glass of wine or a pleasurable meal, Lincoln got from laughter" (Carwardine, 2006, p. 314). Joshua Speed, maybe Lincoln's only true lifelong friend, recalled their days together in Springfield beginning in 1837:

> Mr. Lincoln was a social man, though he did not seek company; it sought him . . . on every winter's night at my store, by a big wood fire, no matter how inclement the weather, eight or ten choice spirits assembled, without distinction of party. It was a sort of social club without organization. They came there because they were sure to find Lincoln. His habit was to engage in conversation on any and all subjects. (Joshua Speed, in Holtzer, 2009, p. 42)

During Lincoln's trials while serving as president, he did develop intimates. He trusted and became professionally close to both Secretary of State Seward and Secretary of War Stanton. And he trusted his two secretaries, John Nicolay and John Hay. Late at night, when Lincoln was working in the White House, he would sometimes break the silence, and the somber mood caused by sad news from the front, by sharing with his secretaries a humorous story or an excerpt from a Shakespearean play. One midnight while Hay was writing in his diary, the president came into his office to read a humorous story to him and Nicolay, "seemingly utterly unconscious that he with his short shirt hanging about his long legs, and setting out behind like the tail feathers of an enormous ostrich, was infinitely funnier than anything in the book he was laughing at" (Thomas, 1952, p. 473).

Ackerman and Maslin-Ostrowski (2004) stress that leaders need people "who are willing to bear witness to their stories. . . . Sharing the burden and vulnerability of leadership can offer solace, hope, and healing" (p. 31).

Heifetz and Linsky (2004) add that it is a mistake to try to be a lone hero, and that alliances help one to build networks to succeed: "Able politicians know . . . [that] the quality of human relationships is more important than almost any other factor in determining results" (p. 35).

Another coping strategy that worked for Lincoln was getting away from the White House. His work schedule did not change, but during the warm Washington summer and fall, the family lived primarily at the Soldiers' Home retreat three miles from the White House. With its cottages and quiet acreage, the retreat offered the president the opportunity to walk with his family, read to the children, and spend time with a small group of friends, or alone. From 1862 to 1864, the first family spent approximately 13 months at the Soldiers' Home, about one-fourth of Lincoln's time as president. Mary Todd Lincoln, writing to a friend, said, "We are truly delighted, with this retreat, the drives and walks around here are delightful, and each day, brings its visitors. Then too, our boy Robert, is with us" (White, 2009, p. 489).

No doubt, Lincoln also took great comfort in his children. However, the early deaths of Edward and Willie must have reminded him of the sadness of losing his mother when he was 9, and his older sister, who died during child-birth when he was 18. Stories of how the Lincolns raised their children indicate they were doting parents. Many stories tell of how the children roamed freely around the White House and, at times, upset adults—but, apparently, not their parents. During the Springfield years, Herndon, out of respect for his older law partner, never told Lincoln how unruly the children were at the law office, where they pulled down books, destroyed pens, ruined inkstands, and scattered papers (Herndon, in Holzer, 2009, pp. 68–69). Lincoln was well aware of how unrestrained the children were but was comfortable with his child-rearing practices (Clinton, 2008). Quite possibly his indulgent paren-tal attitude was intended to contrast with the stark memories of his difficult childhood.

Spiritual Strength

Carwardine (2006, 2008) and White (2009) write quite a bit about Lin-coln's spiritual and religious life. Although Lincoln never officially professed allegiance to a particular religious denomination, his personal moral code, behavior (he did not drink, smoke, or gamble), lifelong opposition to slavery, church attendance, and conversations with religious leaders indicate that he lived within spiritual boundaries. However, most important, Lincoln's extensive use of religious and spiritual language in his public pronouncements— especially during his final years—leave little doubt that he was constantly seeking spiritual answers. Certainly he was greatly influenced by biblical teachings and a belief in divine will. For example, on September 22, 1862, when Lincoln officially issued the Emancipation Proclamation to his cabinet, he stated, according to Secretary of the Navy Gideon Welles, that the victory at Antietam was "an indication of divine will . . . [and that] God has decided this question in favor of the slaves" (Carwardine, 2008, pp. 231–232).

Also, Lincoln's language during the Second Inaugural Address is filled with religious and spiritual references:

- "Both [sides] read the same Bible and pray to the same God."
- ". . . if God wills that [the war] will continue."
- ". . . as was said three thousand years ago, so still it must be said, 'the judgments of the Lord are true and righteous altogether.'"
- "With malice toward none, with charity for all, with firmness in the right as God gives us to see the right."

Carwardine (2008) was particularly impressed with the Second Inaugural Address for its "remarkable absence of self-righteousness" (p. 241). It took courage for Lincoln to state that both sides were responsible for the tragic events of the previous four years. To look for answers to Lincoln's courage and resilience without considering his search for spiritual comfort would be naïve. Because of who he was, Lincoln would continue to reflect and struggle, searching for answers to the great questions of his day. White (2009) concludes, "[Lincoln] also thought into the future, anticipating the moral questions of subsequent generations . . . and underwent a religious odyssey that deepened as he aged, inquiring about everlasting truths until his last day" (p. 676).

All his life Abraham Lincoln was tough—and tender. Maybe even fragile. But he never broke. Why? His actions and writings on the issues of the day supply answers. Lincoln was ambitious and wanted to be remembered, not to gain self-importance, but to make a contribution. His journey begins with a commitment to educate himself, a journey that lasted his whole life. And he gained strength from the tough world of politics, knowing that in the political world one could make a difference on the moral issues of the day. But he also needed a support system that included a network of friends, an appreciation of laughter and wit to balance his melancholy side, and, when in the White House, trusted political allies, a retreat at the Soldiers' Home, the joy of children, and spiritual comfort. But it would be too simple to suggest that the support system made for a smooth journey. Lincoln's road was always rough, and, as president, he carried the weight of the nation. Certainly a reason for his success was the ability to persist, making wise decisions while also suffering under the burden of leadership. Cohen (2002) states

> In war to see things as they are, and not as one would like them to be, to persevere despite disappointments, to know of numerous opportunities lost and of perils still ahead, to lead knowing that one's subordinates and colleagues are in some cases inadequate, in others hostile, is a courage of a rarer kind than a willingness to expose oneself to the unlucky bullet or shell. Without it, all others would be in vain. (p. 224)

Lincoln's Life and Work: Implications for School Leaders

Earlier in this chapter we reviewed several challenges of leadership—making difficult decisions that affect the culture or ethos of an organization, adhering to the mission when confronted with criticism and resistance, and maintaining resilience in the face of personal or professional adversity. These challenges remind us of the inner resources that a school leader must possess to thrive and flourish during difficult times. Lincoln drew upon his personal life story and used internal resources such as patience, lifelong learning, tenacity, character, camaraderie with those he deeply respected, and a genuine desire to make a contribution as he confronted the challenges placed before him. Suffering from bouts of depression as he did, he must have drawn upon spiritual strength, story, and optimism to pull himself from these depths of melancholy.

School leaders are never exempt from challenges. Their decisions—small and large—will, most likely, always be questioned, particularly if they are new to an organization. And many times the leader experiences self-doubt: "Do I have the skills to see this issue through?" So what are some inner resources that school leaders need to stay the course?

Jim Collins (2005) talks about the need to display a paradoxical blend of "personal humility and professional will" (p. 12). Leaders must first and foremost stay focused on the ultimate object of their work—student success, teacher growth, and organizational wellness and excellence. But they must also, as was addressed in Chapter 5, know themselves. Being clear about the focus of their ambitions and their inner strengths and weaknesses is an asset that leaders can draw upon when navigating through difficult situations— especially when "the" answer is not abundantly clear. For example, recently an inner-city school principal related the following dilemma:

> I know from experience that the difference between a good teacher and a poor teacher can amount to a full year of student achievement. And I hold myself and the staff morally accountable, to ensure that every student here succeeds. I've been working all year with a teacher to refine her instructional strategies and knowledge of curriculum and assessment. But I haven't seen a lot of evidence that my supervisory efforts are making a big difference. Don't get me wrong. She is a kind person and has the will to improve her practice. She cares about the students. It's just that her skills are not refined. So my question is "How much longer should I invest in coaching her to improve her practice, given the fact that there are 24 students under her tutelage?" The other difficult dimension of this problem is that the teacher is a single parent. She depends on her teaching salary to live. And I'm not the type simply to transfer her to another school. I really don't know what to do.

This scenario is all too familiar to school leaders. It highlights the moral dilemma of the commitment to promote student success juxtaposed against a commitment to help teachers grow. The subject is a kind, willing teacher who depends on teaching for her livelihood and who is deeply committed to helping students succeed. Yet the career path of students hangs in jeopardy if this teacher's skillfulness does not improve. How much more time can the principal invest, given the urgency of the situation? (And passing the buck to another administrator is not a part of this principal's playbook.)

For guidance through struggles like these, it is helpful for school leaders to create a personal narrative in which the leader states, proactively, what is most important, what cannot be sacrificed—ever. This kind of exercise can provide an anchor of clarity when the sea of uncertainty seems murky and threatens a vision. To get started, leaders might reflect upon and respond in writing to questions such as the following:

- What inspired you to become a school leader?
- How do you define your role as leader?
- What core values and beliefs guide your actions?
- How do people in your organization learn about your character? Your integrity?
- What is your vision or leadership philosophy?
- What do you believe inspires the best in staff?
- How do you provide feedback to others?
- How do you prefer to receive feedback?
- When conflict arises, how do you behave?
- What do you stand for? (Be specific. What evidence would you provide about this?)
- What are your strengths and weaknesses?

Knowing oneself with crystalline clarity gives a leader a firm foundation when faced with negative feedback such as criticism. It provides a platform from which to operate, a reference point.

Recently a principal-teacher leadership team decided to suspend a student for bullying others. In anger, the student launched false claims on the Internet about the principal's and teachers' solicitation of students for amorous encounters. The leadership team became aware of this when a board member contacted the school. The team members sprang into action with statements from their personal narratives and evidence to support their stance. They confronted the student in the presence of his parents and asked him to substantiate his Internet claims. When he could not, they demanded that he take down his false Internet messages and submit a written apology and an explanation of his actions. The team suggested he select a community service project that focused upon developing a sense of empathy for others. The team members were guided in their strategy by their proactive narratives.

Another experience that school leaders encounter is disappointment and failure. For example, a superintendent is fired by a board of education. Or a candidate for the principalship is passed over and another person is selected for the position. How these disappointments are faced profoundly affects what will transpire in the future. Effective school leaders "embrace" failure as an opportunity to start afresh. In the examples just mentioned, the superintendent, although wounded by the rejection of the school board, applied for and was hired by another school board that had an academic focus and whose members perceived their role to be that of "partner" with the superintendent. He and the district are soaring! The candidate for principal, known for her strength in curriculum, was selected as a curriculum director in the same district where she had applied for a principalship. The positive effect of her work is obvious in classrooms across the district.

The constructive response to disappointment or failure has been called "resilience." Resilience is a characteristic of highly effective leaders. It involves developing the capacity to persevere—to be tenacious and to bounce back when the chips are down. One school worked hard all year to raise test scores, and when the test data were reported by the state, they did not show appreciable gains. How did school leaders respond? They developed a celebration called "Let us eat cake." They celebrated their small gains by sharing a large sheet cake and reflected upon the work they did in classrooms to achieve those gains. Then they examined those areas that had not improved. The staff planned what they could do differently to help students improve academically.

Tragedy and disappointment in Lincoln's life developed, within him, a profound sense of compassion for others. They enabled him to deeply understand the pain, suffering, and anguish of the Civil War. When school leaders encounter tragedy or disappointment, they need to take stock of how they are feeling, what they are thinking, and the contextual conditions that were present. Storing away these memories will enable the school leader to draw upon these resources when comforting others who have encountered similar experiences and will equip the leader with the capacity to display empathy.

Effective school leaders possess coping mechanisms for when they become disillusioned. One principal has a picture of a beach on her desk, so she "travels" to the beach—a favorite spot for serenity and reflection—in her head. Another principal takes out a kaleidoscope to change her perspective. Still another principal goes for a brisk walk. Each of these leadership responses conveys an understanding that, when faced with adversity, it is always healthy to change one's perspective and begin anew.

Unfortunately, leaders cannot always forecast the events that befall them. The late Judy Arin Krupp is referenced by Glickman and colleagues (2010, pp. 74–75) in relation to her research on unanticipated events. These events include both personal and professional surprises. Personal unanticipated events are either relationship focused, like an unanticipated divorce; or a health issue, like a sudden heart attack. Professional unanticipated events might involve a job loss due to an economic downturn. The greatest opportunity for change and growth comes when, as a result of an unanticipated event, a transformation of some type occurs that turns a negative experience into a positive one. Two examples illustrate this point.

A school leader was diagnosed and treated for breast cancer. She hit the four-year "survivor" mark and celebrated with friends. When she went in for her annual mammogram, she was told that although there was only a one-half-of-one-percent chance that the cancer would return, it had—this time, on the opposite side. After many sleepless nights full of fear, angry thoughts, "why me" questions, and then a successful second surgery, she awoke one morning and said, "This can control me, or I can control the thoughts that I allow to enter my head. Worry will do nothing but add stress to my life." And so she began exercising, dieting, and pouring herself into her work. Her productivity soared, and her sense of well-being was enhanced.

In the second example, a school leader went to visit his dad. The next day he received a call that his dad had fallen and was hospitalized. Though in his 90s, his dad had always bounced back from health challenges. But this time was the exception; he died. The school leader first found himself in disbelief, and then the grief set in. After the funeral, he had daily thoughts about his dad. He would read an article in the paper and have an immediate impulse to share it with his dad. Then reality set in. He poured himself into his work. His writings and accomplishments—fueled by a sense of sadness but also new-found creativity—became prolific.

Though principals interact with hundreds of people on a weekly basis, theirs is, ironically, often a lonely role, for there is no other like role on campus. As a result, in the loneliness of their office, they often wonder, "Is this the best way I could have handled this?" School leaders who network with other leaders—within and outside the district and on the Internet—can find solace and resources in those connections and enhance their capacity to respond efficiently and effectively to a never-ending array of challenges.

Reflecting on History and the Moment: Implications for the Future

As you reflect upon the key ideas and concepts in this chapter, ponder your own leadership work. Use the space provided to tell a story in which you could be described in either of the following ways:

- Tough, yet tender.
- Resilient, courageous, persistent, or tenacious.

My Leadership Story

Experiment with drafting a personal narrative. What might it say? How might it fuel your efforts to stay focused in the face of unexpected events? Use these questions to guide your effort:

- What brought me here?
- What do I stand for?

Consider incorporating answers to the pertinent questions posed in the earlier discussion of personal narrative as well (see p. 114).

My Personal Narrative

Use this space to jot down any other ideas, insights, or new perspectives from this chapter that you wish to add to your repertoire as a school leader.

CHAPTER EIGHT

Exercising Purposeful Visibility

> Anything that kept the people themselves away from [Lincoln] he
> disapproved—although they nearly annoyed the life out of him by
> unreasonable complaints and requests.
> —John Hay, Lincoln's personal secretary, on the daily White House
> office routine (Burlingame, 2008, Vol. 2, p. 254)

Lincoln lacked executive experience when he became president, and he knew it. After serving some time in office, he stated to his former law partner, Billy Herndon, that "he was entirely ignorant not only of the [presidential] duties, but of the manner of doing the business" (Donald, 1995, p. 285).

Lincoln was a visionary who enjoyed talking about ideas; he was not a manager. During his long Springfield partnership with Herndon, neither Lincoln nor his junior partner was very good at keeping track of expenses or of organizing their legal books and files. Fortunately, Lincoln's personal secretaries (in reality, chief White House assistants), John Nicolay and John Hay, had the managerial skills to keep the "tycoon," as they affectionately called the president, on task. However, in 1861, as the administration was going through the typical growing pains of any new government, it became apparent that Lincoln was developing two executive goals that proved critical to his presidency. First, he was determined to meet with the public face-to-face. Second, he was resolute about visibly engaging with and supporting the troops. As the war evolved, visibly supporting the troops developed into frequent visits to soldiers in camps and hospitals, and significant time spent in the War Department offices.

The Power of Intentional Face-to-Face Interactions

The importance of purposeful face-to-face interaction and visibly observing whether the organization is operating effectively cannot be overstated. Leaders are shaped by the organizational culture and, in turn, help shape the culture when they get out and about (Alvy & Robbins, 1998).

President Lincoln's determination to interact daily with citizens and to visit soldiers in the field helped him assess what was working and what needed changing. Clearly, the president favored a hands-on approach to leadership. Also, his strategy of keeping his face public let citizens and soldiers know that he cared. Not surprisingly, some generals did not appreciate the president's field or headquarter visits. In particular, General McClellan resented the presidential visits, believing Lincoln had no knowledge of military affairs and was simply interfering with his ability to soldier (McPherson, 2008a).

The consequences of Lincoln's executive approach, especially the face-to-face interactions, may have pleased the president, but they often caused havoc in the daily office routine (Burlingame, 2008; Donald, 1995; Oates, 1977; Thomas, 1952). John Hay recalled, "[Lincoln] was extremely unmethodical: it was a four-year struggle on Nicolay's part and mine to get him to adopt some systematic rules" (Burlingame, 2008, Vol. 2, p. 254). But Lincoln was determined to stay in touch with the people. When his leaders did not do the same, his displeasure became known. For example, on September 9, 1861, he wrote a letter expressing his unhappiness with General Fremont's administrative style in Missouri:

> General Fremont needs assistance which is difficult to give him. He is losing the confidence of men near him, whose support any man in his position must have to be successful. His cardinal mistake is that he isolates himself, and allows nobody to see him; and by which he does not know what is going on in the very matter he is dealing with. (Basler, 1953–1955, Vol. IV, p. 513)

McPherson (2008a) adds that Fremont "surrounded himself with a large staff of German and Hungarian soldiers of fortune in gaudy uniforms who turned away many people who had legitimate business with the general" (p. 56). Lincoln clearly wanted his leaders to remain in touch with important stakeholders.

Lincoln's Daily Routine: Visibly Serving the Public

Concerning the daily routine, Lincoln would usually get up early each day, take breakfast (coffee and eggs), read news summaries prepared by his secretaries, and read and sign documents and memos until 10 o'clock in the morning. Then the public would be permitted in. Lincoln called these daily interactions his "public opinion baths." All types of visitors and petitioners would seek to see the president. Meetings were casual and informal, much to the dismay of Nicolay and Hay. Some folks just wanted an autograph or to wish the president good luck. Senators and congressmen would visit and, although they were entitled to move to the front of the line, often had to wait like everyone else. Foreign diplomats, military officers, women appealing military decisions related to their husbands or sons, businessmen, inventors, farmers, everyone and anyone visited with the president (Burlingame, 2008; Donald, 1995). "These visits . . . offered the President an opportunity, in these days before scientific public opinion polling, to get some idea of how ordinary people felt about him and his administration" (Donald, 1995, p. 391). Nicolay and Hay estimated that Lincoln spent about 75 percent of his time meeting with visitors (Phillips, 1992). Citizens appreciated the president's patient listening, kindness, and lack of pomp. Commenting on the visitors, Lincoln said, "They do not want much . . . and they get very little. . . . I know how I would feel in their place" (Thomas, 1952, p. 457).

Twice a week Lincoln had cabinet meetings in the afternoons, so the visits ended at lunch. When there were no scheduled meetings, Lincoln would continue to see the public in the afternoon. The president was often exhausted at the end of each day, but the meetings kept him in touch with the people and reduced the levels of bureaucracy and red tape. Citizens appreciated the effort. Word traveled about the president's thoughtfulness and consideration during these open meetings, affirming the public sobriquet "Father Abraham" and the belief, for many, that all would be well. To alleviate the president's exhaustion and keep him healthy, Mrs. Lincoln would often bring the meetings to a close by insisting that he get some fresh air.

> So, almost every day at four o'clock, unless bad weather interfered, the coachman brought a carriage to the White House portico, and the President and his wife went for a drive. They often stopped at some hospital, where Lincoln walked from cot to cot, taking the wan hands in friendly grip, joking with the convalescents and offering cheer and comfort to those with more serious hurts. He was especially solicitous to the friendless Southern boys. (Thomas, 1952, p. 470)

Using State-of-the-Art Technology to Network Effectively

Lincoln's use of the telegraph became a crucial tool during the war (Cohen, 2002; McPherson, 2008b). "Next door to Stanton's office, the telegraph room was a refuge for Lincoln, who would pay almost daily visits to read dispatches from the front and to compose replies" (Cohen, 2002, p. 28). Aside from the White House and the Soldiers' Home, Lincoln spent more time at the War Department telegraph office than anywhere else. He would often telegraph generals at the front, engaging in real-time "conversation." The telegraph enabled Lincoln to be "visible" to the generals and pursue his hands-on approach to leadership. This tool enabled Lincoln to break away from the White House bubble, to know what was taking place in the field. Lincoln was determined to face the truth, whether that truth brought victory or defeat. If the Union were going to be defeated, it would not be because the president kept his head in the sand. To illustrate, consider these inquiring telegrams sent by Lincoln to his generals (on June 24, 28, and 30); and finally to the nation (on July 4), related to the Battle of Gettysburg (July 1–3, 1863):

> Have you any reports of the enemy moving in Pennsylvania? And if any, what? (June 24)

> What news now? What are the enemy firing at four miles from your works? (June 28)

I judge by absence of news that the enemy is not crossing, or pressing up to the Susquehanna. Please tell me what you know of his movements. (June 30)

July 4th, 10. A. M. 1863.

The President announces to the country that news from the Army of the Potomac [in Gettysburg], up to 10 P. M. of the 3rd is such as to cover that Army with the highest honor, to promise a great success to the cause of the Union, and to claim the condolence of all for the gallant men fallen. And that for this, he especially desires that on this day, He whose will, not ours, should ever be done, be everywhere remembered and reverenced with profoundest gratitude.

—Abraham Lincoln

(The announcement was a "press release" sent by telegraph from the War Department.) (Basler, 1953–1955, Vol. VI, pp. 293, 299, 310, 314)

Purposeful Visibility: Working with the Military

The most important exercise of the president's visibility strategy related to the time he spent with the military. Lincoln left Washington 11 times during his presidency to visit the Army of the Potomac, totaling 42 days (McPherson, 2008b). In Washington he sought out soldiers on his rides and walks and his visits to hospitals, almost on a daily basis. Lincoln is the only president to visit a battlefield while fighting was taking place. (Whether it was wise for him to do so is another matter!) Oates (1977) describes one such incident:

> On July 12 [1864] Lincoln stood on the parapet at Fort Stevens, watching as Union and rebel forces fired away at one another. He saw a body of Union soldiers move across shimmering summer fields and drive the rebels from a house and an orchard with muskets smoking. By now rebel sharpshooters were sniping at Fort Stevens, but Lincoln stood there oblivious to the bullets whizzing around him, and a soldier fell at his side. Finally, an officer made the President get down before he was killed. (p. 394)

Visiting military camps was not just about supporting the soldiers. Lincoln used the time to size up his generals, press his position on military strategy (it was about defeating armies, not occupying cities), gauge whether military resources were sufficient, and assess the morale of the soldiers. Visibility, of course, is a two-way street. The time in camp gave the generals and the soldiers a chance to ask questions of the president and measure the man who was leading the war effort. The following accounts are two examples of the president's visibility strategy.

In April 1863, the president decided to visit General Hooker for five days in Falmouth, Virginia, about a mile from Lee's army across the Rappahannock River. Lincoln brought his family and some aides with him. Through field glasses Lincoln could see the destruction that had taken place at Fredericksburg. He reviewed Hooker's 130,000 troops and spent much time talking with Hooker about strategy. Lincoln was a little uneasy with the level of confidence that Hooker displayed in their conversations—he sounded too much like McClellan. While in Falmouth, Lincoln "lived in a large tent with his family, spoke with the wounded in nearby hospital tents . . . attended gala troop reviews . . . [and] in a mule-drawn ambulance . . . bounced around the camp visiting with the men" (Oates, 1977, p. 346).

McPherson (2008a) describes a formidable example of Lincoln's role as a visible commander in chief, during the military operations at Norfolk, Virginia, in May 1862. In this situation, Lincoln was directly involved, *on site*, in real-time military decisions (again, it may not have been the most prudent strategy in terms of a president's personal security). The president's action proved decisive to the success of the Union's maneuvers. On May 7, Lincoln

> took direct operational control of a drive to capture Norfolk and to push a gunboat fleet up the James River. Lincoln ordered Gen. John Wool, commander at Fort Monroe, to land troops on the south bank of Hampton Roads. The president even personally carried out a reconnaissance to select the best landing spot. (McPherson, 2008a, p. 89)

Military camp visits, talking with soldiers, and having an opportunity to engage directly in decisions as commander in chief invigorated the president. Lincoln knew that he was personally making a difference. Following the May

1862 Norfolk operation, close associates of the president commented that his own morale seemed boosted by the activities and that he hadn't looked as healthy since the March 1861 inauguration.

Visibility, Reflection, and Intentional Decision Making

As noted in Chapter 7, Abraham Lincoln knew his own story. He knew that those born without privilege must take action to change the course of their lives. He applied that same philosophy to the nation. Taking action was the way he managed as president. But the actions were not precipitous; impulsivity was not in Lincoln's character. He moved forward after engaging in dialogue, after listening (for example, engaging in his "public opinion baths"), observing, and reflecting on the local context of the issue; and then assessing the situation within the greater national framework. Thus, his visibility was *intentional*. Furthermore, Lincoln's leadership approach was fueled by human engagement. His public manner, how he behaved with others—his humility and ability to listen actively—was a result of his life experiences. The humility was critical to the success of Lincoln's conversational style. His manner enabled others to be vulnerable in his presence, and it enabled him to connect with each stratum of society. The evidence indicates that he quickly made an assessment of those with whom he met. These skills enabled him to remain in touch with reality and face the hard decisions with accurate data. Without accurate data, faulty decisions are made. The nation and the president could not afford that possibility. In *The Heart Aroused*, poet and essayist David Whyte (1994) shares insights about the human experience that can help us understand the essence of, and rationale for, Lincoln's leadership approach—an approach that depended on observation and dialogue: "The tradition tells us again and again that amid the complexities of the world, exactly what we have, exactly our experiences, is the only place we can start" (p. 254).

Lincoln's Life and Work: Implications for School Leaders

This chapter has reviewed Lincoln's strategic use of visibility—to stay in touch with citizens, to demonstrate support for troops, to communicate care, to assess generals' competence, to shape culture, and to be accessible. His visibility was characterized by humility, and his manner enabled others to be vulnerable in his presence. Lincoln used observation and dialogue to stay in touch with reality and to face hard decisions with accurate data.

In examining Lincoln's practices at a national level, one is struck by the number of parallels that can be drawn with the work of school leaders in local contexts. Lincoln's lack of executive experience, for instance, is reminiscent of the reality of the new leader. That is, one can never be totally prepared for the events that transpire. The element of surprise is part of the job. A high school principal recently related a story of students rushing into his office with the news that "a man was running around the football field naked!" The principal grabbed his walkie-talkie and, as he ran to the field, contacted the school resource officer. Within minutes the local police appeared and subdued the man, who had escaped from a local hospital. An athletic coach, in the meantime, had skillfully cleared the players from the field and reported that "there were lots of jokes, but everything was cool." "Nothing in my administrative coursework could have prepared me for this," the principal reflected, as he walked to his office to prepare a communication about the incident to parents, students, and community members.

Similarly, teacher leaders often feel a lack of preparedness for events that unfold at the school and classroom levels, as illustrated in this example. A senior student frequently complained about headaches. She had been checked by the family's physician, who could find nothing wrong. Then, while on a field trip, the student suffered an aneurism and later tragically died. "Nothing in my coursework prepared me for the grief counseling I found myself doing with students and the parents of the young lady who died," the teacher leader tearfully noted. The lack of preparedness for surprises and unanticipated events, and the huge emotional demands place leaders in a difficult position, at best. What general advice can be given to school leaders to cope when unanticipated events occur? Here's one observation:

> A few days after September 11th, many of the top executives in the New York area were asked to give advice concerning how to cope with such overwhelming tragedy. "Their wisdom, distilled, came down to four basic truisms: be calm, tell the truth, put people before business, then

get back to business as soon as possible." (Wayne and Kaufman [2001, September 16, pp. 1, 4)] . . . [School leaders] need to know that during a crisis the staff will look to them for action, direction, support, security, composure, and hope. (Robbins & Alvy, 2004, p. 222)

Lincoln used purposeful visibility to remain situationally aware. Interestingly, in a Mid-continent Research for Education and Learning (McREL) study, *School Leadership That Works* (Waters, Marzano, & McNulty, 2004), two important questions were addressed:

Do the focus and quality of leadership have a significant relationship to student achievement? What specific leadership responsibilities and practices have the greatest impact? (pp. 48–49)

The researchers reached the following conclusions. "Leadership matters. McREL found a significant, positive correlation between effective school leadership and student achievement" (p. 49). Twenty-one key areas of leadership responsibility were identified. The study also led researchers to conclude that "effective leaders not only know what to do, but how, when, and why to do it" (p. 49). Several of the key areas of leadership responsibility identified are reflective of behaviors associated with Lincoln. School leaders who practice these responsibilities, often in an interrelated manner, are more likely to succeed at promoting student achievement and organizational success.

Let's explore a few of these areas of responsibility. Lincoln was visible to the general public; to troops in the field, camps, and hospitals; and to military leaders. His presence communicated care, accessibility, and assessment. School leaders can follow this example and practice purposeful visibility. When principals, superintendents, teacher leaders, instructional coaches, and assistant principals spend time in classrooms, for example, rather than in their respective offices, they send a strong message that the center of the schoolhouse is where student learning is taking place. Further, these visits provide observation-based data about the quality of instruction, student learning, expectations, climate, and school culture that can, in turn, inform future decisions. In addition, visits such as these can build schoolwide norms of practice. What school leaders focus on during these visits sends a strong message to organizational members about what is important. For instance, if during classroom visits, students' active participation is the object of the observation, organizational members will quickly notice that that is a core value. But leaders' presence in classrooms, hallways, the gym, athletic fields, the lunchroom, parking lots, or media center also communicate the messages "I care about what is going on here" and "I am accessible," in addition to simply providing a strategy for data collection.

Organizational culture, or "the way we do things around here," influences leaders' behavior. It spells out, for instance, what's appropriate to talk about in the faculty room—and what's not. However, leaders can also shape the culture of the school or district by what they pay attention to, celebrate, allocate time or resources for, or reward. In many schools or districts, expanding leadership roles to include teacher leaders has had a profound effect on the culture, making it more participatory. And culture can inform action. For example, knowing who the informal power brokers in the culture are provides leaders with information about whom they should go to in order to test out ideas regarding potential changes in the organization.

Simple actions—such as greeting students as they get off the buses or out of cars—carry profound significance because of culture. Reading and responding to cultural clues can leverage one's investment of time. For example, while greeting students can, on the surface, appear to be a behavior that builds relationships and provides a sense of order, it also provides an opportunity for outreach to parents, students, and community members. Being "out there"— whether in academic or nonacademic spaces—provides leaders with a sense of "situational awareness," the leadership responsibility on the list of 21 in the McREL study with the highest correlation to student achievement. Observations and dialogue keep leaders in touch with situations and provide accurate data for making difficult decisions.

The work lives of school leaders are said to be characterized by "brevity, fragmentation, and variety" (Peterson, 1982, pp. 1–4). That is, most of their tasks last nine minutes or less. They experience a sense of fragmentation, because they are often interrupted by forces over which they have no control. And the tasks in which they engage are varied in terms of both the type and the emotional demands they present to the leader. In *The New Principal's*

Fieldbook (Robbins & Alvy, 2004), we offer a strategy to make the "brevity, fragmentation, and variety" actually work for school leaders.

Principals can find ways to inspire teacher reflection, gain a sense of the taught curriculum, develop a knowledge of the climate of classrooms and the general emotional health of the school, build relationships with staff and students, build schoolwide norms of practice, and enhance storytelling capacity through a strategy called Leading and Learning By Wandering Around (LLBWA).* This strategy uses fragmentation as an opportunity. It involves using short time segments—some planned, some unplanned—to get out of the office and into classrooms or campus areas to observe. Some principals make a doorknob hanger for the office that reads "Out Learning" while they are doing LLBWA. This little sign sends a strong message to anyone who comes looking for the principal that this is a top-priority task! There are many approaches to LLBWA. Here are a few.

An approach known as "8-10-12-2-4" simply means the principal visits classrooms or the campus at 8 a.m., 10 a.m., noon, 2 p.m., and 4 p.m. on selected days. These visits can be made with teacher leaders as long as staff recognize that the visits are not for evaluation purposes. Visits provide several types of information, as the principal and the teacher leader reflect upon questions such as these:

- How do teachers begin classes? By engaging students immediately in a meaningful activity or just taking roll?
- How do classes conclude? (Hopefully, with an activity that invites students to summarize their learning.)
- What is the nature of the taught curriculum (versus that which is tested)?
- What do transitions look like?
- How does instruction in the morning compare to instruction in the afternoon?
- What happens in the cafeteria?

---

* Information in this section on LLBWA is adapted from Robbins and Alvy, 2004, pp. 125–129.

- What procedures protect academic learning time? What should be put into action? Are there logjams at passing periods? Why or why not?
- Who lingers after school? Why?
- Are the goals of the school improvement plans being implemented?

A few other strategies used during LLBWA include the following:

- Conducting student interviews—to gain the students' perspective of the classroom
- Parent outreach calls—made when observing positive student behaviors, to build positive home-school relationships and celebrate student success
- Collecting student work samples—to assess the quality of work assigned to students, the content addressed, student interest, values, and expectations for performance
- Seven-minute classroom snapshots—to quickly assess curriculum, instruction, and assessment in action
- Post-it feedback—to succinctly describe what is observed during walk-through visits.

Again, these visits can be made with teacher leaders, or teacher leaders can make these visits on their own as long as the school's cultural norms support positive professional interaction.

Principals report several benefits from implementing LLBWA, including the following:

- Early warnings about problems
- An avenue to celebrate success
- Knowledge about the congruence between desired or agreed-on behaviors and actual behaviors
- Increased storytelling capacity
- Elevated staff awareness of key cultural values and beliefs
- Greater principal believability and clout
- An expanded sense of control
- Sanity—the pleasure of being out and about
- Increased contact with students

Principals using LLBWA share one caution: it's important to communicate with staff about what you are doing and why you are doing it, lest your actions be construed as "bed checks."

And finally, it's not just what school leaders do that's important, it's also the tone in which they do it. As was mentioned earlier, Lincoln's humility, his manner, enabled others to be vulnerable in his presence. School leaders must consider questions such as these: How can I encourage people to be at ease in my presence? To let their rough edges show? To share their concerns or frailties? Only when a comfort level exists can school leaders genuinely move forward in the partnership and quest to promote staff and student learning.

Reflecting on History and the Moment: Implications for the Future

Visibility, humility, relationship building, accessibility. The list of leadership behaviors requisite for student and school success is daunting. Yet we now know more than ever before about which practices and what components make a difference. The Student Learning Nexus, Figure 8.1, graphically depicts the components of classroom practice that promote student learning (Alvy & Robbins, 2009; Robbins & Alvy, 2009).

Please take a moment to examine the model in Figure 8.1 and consider the following questions, using the space beneath each question to jot down your thoughts.

- Would you add to the model?

(questions continued on p. 133)

Figure 8.1

The Student Learning Nexus:
Aligning Instruction, Curriculum, and Assessment in a Healthy Environment

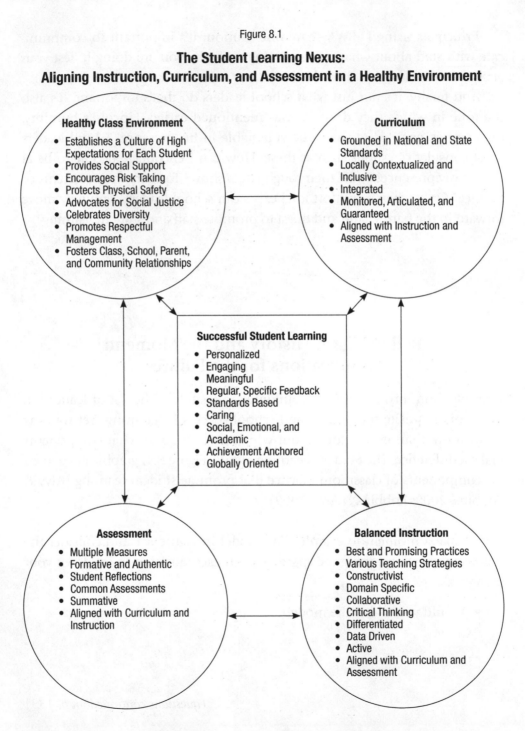

- How do you support and nurture these components as the leader?

- How might an LLBWA visit focus on one of these components?

- How might the components stimulate dialogue during a walk-through, instructional rounds, peer observation, conversation about student work, or development of a school improvement plan?

- What would need to go on at a school level to promote these vibrant components of classroom practice?

Use this space to jot down any other ideas, insights, or new perspectives from this chapter that you wish to add to your repertoire as a school leader.

CHAPTER NINE

Demonstrating Personal Growth and Enhanced Competence as a Lifelong Learner, Willing to Reflect on and Expand Ideas

> The failure to recognize the attributes of flexibility and *the capacity for growth* in Lincoln and, instead, to treat him as a static, stunted figure is to misuse the legacy that he has left for all of us.
> —John Hope Franklin, February 12, 1985, emphasis added

"The capacity for growth" is a cornerstone of the Lincoln legacy and the reason why teaching is a "calling." After all, the purpose of teaching is to help students achieve their maximum capacity for growth. *The Lincoln example is especially inspirational to educators because his desire to gain knowledge and wisdom never faded.* Whether one examines the works of historians such as John Hope Franklin or Lincoln's supporters and critics, almost all agree that his achievements resulted from a lifetime of unrelenting personal growth. For example, newspaper publisher Horace Greeley, often a severe presidential critic, reluctantly came to appreciate Lincoln. Consider his assessment:

> [Lincoln] was not born king of men, ruling by the restless might of his natural superiority, but a child of the people, who made himself a great persuader, therefore a leader, by dint of firm resolve, and patient effort, and dogged perseverance.... There was probably no year of his life in which he was not a wiser, cooler, better man than he had been the year preceding. (Greeley, in Holzer, 2009, pp. 111–112)

In this observation, Greeley defines personal growth and lifetime learning for us. Isn't this what we all strive for—to have others say, "You are a better and wiser person than you were last year"?

This singular aspect of Lincoln's character, the desire to learn and improve as a person and a leader, is what initially prompted us as authors to see why it would be important for educators to study Lincoln's life and leadership example. Lincoln's story is not only about his historical narrative. For educators, it is also about the power of learning to change lives. However, in all fairness, educators must remember that Lincoln accomplished his goals without formal schooling; his accomplishments were a "stunning work of self-education" (Miller, 2002, p. 44). Yes, he had a few mentors along the way, mostly legal acquaintances; but the mentors were not classroom teachers. This is, of course, one of the most intriguing aspects of his journey. The lesson here is to remember, always, that children have a natural desire to learn, and to "lose" a student, regardless of the reason, and to lose that student's possibility for growth, is a heartbreaking ending, as we know from our contemporary high school dropout crisis.

Personal Growth and the Role of Group Support

Lincoln enjoyed the camaraderie of the group and sharing ideas with others. As educators, we constantly refer to learning communities (Bennis & Nanus, 1985; Cotton, 2003; DuFour & Eaker, 1998; Newmann & Wehlage, 1995; Senge, 1990). In their classic study of 90 top leaders, Bennis and Nanus (1985) follow up on Burns's (1978) groundbreaking work on transformational leadership by emphasizing that transformational leaders are "superb listener[s] . . . and great askers, and they do pay attention" (p. 96). Bennis and Nanus's research also stresses that effective leaders are "perpetual learners"; they "talked about learning," "learn[ed] from experience," and served as powerful models for others (pp. 188, 205). Commenting specifically on schools, Cotton (2003) emphasizes that role modeling as a learner is critical to a leader's success and that in high-achieving schools the expectation of continuous improvement by the staff is a norm that "has been found by researchers since the early days of the principal-as-instructional-leader research" (p. 29). Today, the power and energy of the professional learning community is greatly enhanced by the teacher leadership movement, which extends the modeling of the learning leader to every corner of a school.

President Lincoln's life models the conceptualization of the leader as a learner and the importance of maintaining a learning community that builds capacity. Consider Lincoln's choice of cabinet members, as so expertly discussed in Goodwin's (2005) *Team of Rivals*. Lincoln's goal was to bring the best on board and let them work autonomously, based on their expertise. His intent was not to hover over them. The cabinet members had autonomy unless their work hindered the overall mission. And although the relationships were rocky at times, as we noted in Chapter 3, Lincoln's preference was to let his team work the problems out. Lincoln also wanted his team members, and others with whom he worked, to let him know how his own performance could improve. This attitude is critical to establishing team trust and team capacity building. To illustrate, in Chapter 2 we discussed how Lincoln sought assistance when writing his First Inaugural Address in 1861; most of the memorable last paragraph was the work of Secretary of State Seward. In an 1861 conversation, Lincoln reached out to a political rival by stating, "When you see me doing anything that for the good of the country ought not to be done, come and tell me so, and why you think so" (Goodwin, 2005, p. 369).

A Personal Example of Lifelong Learning

Throughout his life, Lincoln impressed colleagues and built trusting friendships through his example of being a lifelong learner. As Lincoln traveled the Eighth Judicial Circuit in the 1840s and 1850s, colleagues marveled at his capacity to learn. Fellow lawyer Leonard Swett remembered, "Life to [Lincoln] was a school . . . and he was always studying and mastering every subject which came before him" (Goodwin, 2005, p. 369). Lincoln's range and appetite for learning were boundless. While traveling on the prairie, he read Lord Byron, Robert Burns, Shakespeare (especially enjoying *Richard III, Julius*

Caesar, *Macbeth*, and *Hamlet*), and, for mental exercise, the six volumes of Euclid's Mathematical Theorems. Interestingly, in a campaign piece he helped write for a journalist during the 1860 presidential election, Lincoln explained his Euclidian experience as part of a sincere desire to continue learning. Writing about Lincoln in the third person, the journalist stated, "He studied and nearly mastered the Six-books of Euclid since he was a member of Congress. He regrets his want of education, and does what he can to supply the want" (Basler, 1953–1955, Vol. IV, p. 62). Again, we hear Lincoln's humble voice. He was not about to say that he had completely mastered Euclid, nor that his education was satisfactory.

As we have mentioned several times, Lincoln periodically suffered from depression. The arts, Shakespeare, a satirical essay, a humorous anecdote, an entertaining magician, or attending the theater all helped the president (and Mrs. Lincoln) cope with the difficult times. The following letter to a Shakespearean actor who performed for the president provides a glimpse into how Lincoln momentarily escaped the reality of wartime. The president's enthusiasm for Shakespeare and his characteristic lifelong learning qualities make the letter particularly pertinent:

> For one of my age, I have seen very little of the drama. The first presentation of Falstaff I ever saw was yours here, last winter or spring. I am very anxious to see it again. Some of Shakespeare's plays I have never read; while others I have gone over perhaps as frequently as any unprofessional reader. Among the latter are Lear, Richard Third, Henry Eighth, Hamlet, and especially Macbeth. I think nothing equals Macbeth. It is wonderful. Unlike you gentlemen of the profession, I think the soliloquy in Hamlet commencing "O, my offence is rank" surpasses that commencing "To be, or not to be." But pardon the small attempt at criticism.
>
> —A. Lincoln
> (Basler, 1953–1955, Vol. VI, p. 392)

After entering the White House, practical considerations forced Lincoln to study military strategy. The president would go to the Library of Congress, pick out books, and spend long evenings studying military history. McPherson (2009) notes that after the bombardment of Fort Sumter, Lincoln "faced a steep learning curve as commander in chief," but by 1862 he was up to the challenge (p. 34). McPherson adds the following:

> [Lincoln] observed the successes and failures of his own and the enemy's military commanders and drew apt conclusions; he made mistakes and learned from them; he applied his large quotient of common sense to slice through the obfuscations and excuses of military subordinates. (p. 34)

An examination of Lincoln's correspondence and the observations of those who saw him in action throughout the years provide a fascinating portrait of his philosophy of learning, self-reliant attitude, and approach to the formation of ideas. A letter that Lincoln wrote in 1855 to a prospective lawyer who sought to study with him provides a compelling description of how Lincoln viewed learning. After stating that he would be unable to tutor because of extended time on the circuit, Lincoln offered the following advice:

> If you are resolutely determined to make a lawyer of yourself, the thing is more than half done already. It is but a small matter whether you read *with* any body or not. I did not read with any one. Get the books, and read and study them till you understand them in their principal features; and that is the main thing. It is of no consequence to be in a large town while you are reading. I read at New-Salem, which never had three hundred people living in it. The *books*, and your *capacity* for understanding them are just the same in all places. . . . Always bear in mind that your own resolution to succeed, is more important than any other one thing. (Basler, 1953–1955, Vol. II, p. 327, emphasis in original)

For Lincoln, the importance of self-determination—the burning desire to learn—cannot be overemphasized. Lincoln's success at learning without assistance is also a prominent feature of the letter. What is most intriguing is his advice concerning where to study. Lincoln does not take the position that one must be in a big city to learn; books are the key, and one's own capacity to learn.

Lincoln greatly admired Senator Henry Clay, the famous Whig politician who died on June 29, 1852. Lincoln was a Whig before becoming a Republican in the mid-1850s (he changed parties primarily because of his opposition to the expansion of slavery). His political philosophy was greatly influenced by Clay. On July 6, 1852, Lincoln gave a eulogy for Clay in Springfield. One section in particular is insightful concerning Lincoln the man, and his educational philosophy:

> Mr. Clay's education, to the end of his life, was comparatively limited. I say *"to the end of his life,"* because I have understood that, from time to time, he added something to his education during the greater part of his whole life. Mr. Clay's lack of a more perfect early education, however it may be regretted generally, teaches at least one profitable lesson; it teaches that in this country, one can scarcely be so poor, but that, if he *will*, he *can* acquire sufficient education to get through the world respectably. (Basler, 1953–1955, Vol. II, p. 124, emphasis in original)

This is an interesting section. Lincoln is clearly hinting at parallels between his experience with education and Clay's experience. Again, self-determination is essential to success: "if he *will*, he *can*." This segment is also making a case for lifelong learning: "from time to time, he added something to his education." Although it is not overstated, the eulogy segment implies, optimistically, that a little education can bring you respect and success.

Advancing Individual Thinking and the Thinking of the Nation

An important point to consider beyond Lincoln's success at self-education and pursuit of lifelong learning is how he continued to expand and reconceptualize his ideas and, as a result, help the nation expand its mission. For example, Lincoln may have opposed slavery throughout his life, but until changing his position in 1863 he was unwilling to let go of the constitutional "right" of certain states to hold slaves. An interesting question to ask is this: What kind of reflective process did Lincoln go through when mulling over ideas? As we consider what Lincoln had to say about his own thought process, it is important to keep in mind Miller's (2002) insightful observation that in our contemporary world, intelligence is often equated with speed of thought. To his lifelong friend, Joshua Speed, Lincoln once remarked, "I am slow to learn, and slow to forget that which I have learned. My mind is like a piece of steel—very hard to scratch anything on it, and almost impossible thereafter to rub it out" (Miller, 2002, pp. 13–14).

Lincoln's remarks are especially enlightening when we examine a conversation that Lincoln had at the White House with Frederick Douglass on August 10, 1863. In the excerpt just quoted Lincoln admits that it takes him a while to absorb an idea—speed of thought and speed of comprehension were not in his nature. However, once an idea settled with him, it remained with him. In the following episode, Douglass asked for a presidential meeting to protest the pay differential between black and white troops, the inability of black soldiers to be commissioned as officers, and the need for Union troops to retaliate when black soldiers or prisoners of war were summarily executed (Burlingame, 2008; Goodwin, 2005; White, 2009). Douglass was making his first trip to the executive mansion and wasn't sure if the president would see him. When he entered the White House, Douglass was escorted in to see Lincoln within minutes, although the executive mansion was crowded with citizens seeking the president's attention. Lincoln and Douglass greeted each other respectfully, and they had a frank conversation on the issues. Before Douglass left, the president mentioned that he had read a recent speech by Douglass accusing the president of being slow and vacillating. The president agreed with Douglass's assessment that he arrived at conclusions very deliberately, but he disagreed with the criticism related to vacillation (Goodwin, 2005; Miller, 2002). Lincoln said, "Mr. Douglass, I do not think the charge can be sustained; I think it cannot be shown that when I have once taken a position, I have ever retreated from it" (Miller, 2002, p. 14). Again the "quickness" issue surfaces. Lincoln is deliberative about *learning* new ideas (in the Joshua Speed episode), and deliberative about *acting* on the ideas (in the Frederick Douglass episode). A fair question to ask is this: How would Lincoln fare in today's world of instant "everything"? The question raises important issues concerning the risks for our society if thoughtful reflection is not valued.

A final point about Lincoln's reflective process relates to how he teased out valued ideas when writing. In the 1800s it was very common for "experts" to give lengthy lectures to audiences as a form of intellectual entertainment.

Lincoln tried his hand at it with mixed success. He lectured several times on the history and importance of "Discoveries and Inventions." During the lecture he concludes, *"Writing*—the art of communicating thoughts to the mind, through the eye—is the great invention of the world" (Basler, 1953–1955, Vol. III, p. 390). What makes this definition so interesting is the simplicity of Lincoln's words in clarifying a principle that is vital to our modern understanding of the writing process—writing is a recursive activity in which thinking and writing interact, enhancing the development of more complex ideas. Thomas Eckert, the chief of the War Department telegraph office, describes how Lincoln applied this principle in Eckert's office. Eckert maintained that if Lincoln wanted privacy when writing, he would visit Eckert's office for some peace and quiet. In June 1862, Lincoln visited Eckert's office almost every day to work on a document. According to Eckert,

> [Lincoln] would look out the window a while and then put his pen to paper, but he did not write much at once. He would study between times and when he had made up his mind he would put down a line or two, and then sit quiet for a few minutes. After a time he would resume his writing, only to stop again at intervals [to check telegrams relating to the war]. . . . This he did nearly every day for several weeks. . . . Sometimes he would not write more than a line or two, and once I observed that he had put question-marks on the margins of what he had written. He would read over each day all the matter he had previously written and revise it, studying carefully each sentence. (Eckert in Holzer, 2009, pp. 235–236)

The document that Lincoln was working on was the Emancipation Proclamation.

Miller (2002) reminds us, "Abraham Lincoln was not born, after all, on Mount Rushmore" (p. 54). Thus, what makes Lincoln's ascent to Rushmore so compelling is that he was not born with the advantages of the other three presidential figures enshrined on the monument—Washington, Jefferson, and Theodore Roosevelt. That distinction does not diminish the accomplishments of the other three presidents; each one has earned his sacred place in United States history. In fact, what makes the accomplishments of Washington, Jefferson, and Roosevelt so impressive is that they could have lived quiet lives of privilege but chose not to do so. Lincoln's climb was, of course, different. He was not exposed to the ideas of the world and an education of advantage at an early age. Self-education was the vehicle that brought Lincoln success. When he achieved a degree of success at each stage of his life, *he chose to study more.* Lifelong learning and reflection enabled Lincoln to see not only the ideas of his day, but also a new future that would expand the American dream. "As our case is new, so we must think anew, and act anew. We must disenthrall ourselves, and then we shall save the country."

Lincoln's Life and Work: Implications for School Leaders

Lincoln's example of lifelong learning serves as an inspiration for contemporary school leaders. Learning broadens horizons, affords additional perspectives, and provides the resources of multiple thoughts to enrich our work. Writing, in turn, allows us to put our experiences, and the connection we've made with formal and informal works and with individuals (famous and not), into words so that we may reflect upon them and share them with others.

School leaders make conscious choices about their capacity to grow by the activities in which they choose to engage. When health reasons forced a consultant to cancel a weeklong training on powerful teaching strategies for staff in the Saluda School District in South Carolina, the superintendent, Dr. David Mathis, stepped in and agreed to teach the class himself. He did this because learning is a priority for him, and the Saluda School District and teachers had committed time on their calendars. The superintendent spent hours reading and going over lesson plans on the phone with the consultant. Months later, when the consultant conducted a site visit, it was obvious that Dr. Mathis had taught the content in a way that was highly effective, given the number of staff members who were using the teaching strategies in their daily practice to foster student learning.

School leaders who are committed to learning manifest that commitment in strategic ways. Those who observe them in action often follow their example and, in turn, influence others in the organization. To illustrate, superintendent Tom Narak works in a "good school district . . . that he wants to make great" (von Frank, 2009, p. 1) in West Des Moines, Iowa. Narak regularly turns to a single-page document on his desk known as his individual personal learning plan. "It's easy for other things to come up," Narak said. "My challenge is to make sure I devote myself to areas where the final results are really important, dedicate the necessary resources, and look for more tangible connections to student learning" (p. 1). The personal learning plan that Narak created focused on improving student achievement through effective instructional and assessment practices, with a specific goal of closing the achievement gap:

> He set four leadership goals, including becoming involved in activities to promote cultural proficiency and developing a plan to recruit and maintain minority faculty, and three learning goals including working more closely with his board and resource people. He identified indicators of progress, set start and end dates for each goal, and specified when he would review his progress. (von Frank, 2009, p. 6)

Reflecting on the benefits of the individual learning plan, Narak said it "helps district leaders model professional learning for site-based leaders, from principal to teachers. . . . It's all about accountability and being results based. . . . The professional learning plan is a way you can really measure and show you've accomplished what you set out to do."

School leaders model learning in many contexts. For example, leaders learn on the job by conducting book studies, lesson studies, or article reviews. Such activities provide a way to engage others in learning communities, to focus on topics that add to one's repertoire and foster learning. What is essential in every learning forum is that what is read or studied has a direct link to enhancing practice and its result, student success. The shared focus on a specific source, such as articles on preparing staff and students for the 21st century, influences dialogue within and across the organization. It also causes practitioners to reflect upon current practices and identify what they should keep doing, stop doing, and start doing.

Another context in which school leaders model learning on the job is in the classroom. That is, as a result of spending time observing in classrooms, school leaders learn about which teaching strategies have the greatest effect on student learning. They also discover what learning looks like on a school-wide basis and how teachers differ in their delivery of instruction. Spending time in classrooms also affords school leaders an opportunity to participate in student groups and learn how students are perceiving the learning process. In schools that operate as professional learning communities, another source of learning for school leaders is the time spent on data analysis teams or on teams dedicated to mapping the curriculum or developing common assessments.

Formal ways of learning for school leaders can include university coursework and online classes. The Internet provides a valuable array of social networking resources. Chat rooms, Web sites, and blogs create opportunities for school leaders to network and dialogue with others all over the world. Conference sessions and professional development institutes sponsored by professional associations provide opportunities for school leaders to learn from researchers, consultants, and practitioners and to learn by networking with others. Often as a result of these experiences, school leaders do "turnaround training," sharing their learning with staff members. The McREL study mentioned in Chapter 8 found that a leadership responsibility closely linked with student learning was "intellectual stimulation." After reading the research by Waters et al. (2004), one principal routinely challenged herself to provide "intellectual stimulation" beyond formal professional development days by using faculty meetings for learning opportunities. She also included a short summary of research in every "week in review" publication that she and her leadership team distributed, summarizing the highlights of the week at school.

Within professional learning communities, it is a cultural norm that all members commit to learning about learning—both within the schoolhouse and with the community at large. In this context, school leaders are the "head learners" (DuFour, 2001). DuFour writes:

> I have come to understand the most significant contribution a principal can make to developing others is creating an appropriate context for adult learning. It's context—the programs, procedures, beliefs, expectations, and habits that constitute the norm for a given school—that plays

the largest role in determining whether professional development efforts will have an impact on that school. (p. 14)

Roland Barth (personal communication, 2007, Miami Dade Leadership Retreat) pointed out the strong relationship between staff and student learning when he said, "I've yet to see the school where the learning curves of students are upward and the learning curves of adults are downward. Learning goes hand-in-hand or it doesn't go at all." In an informal sense, school leaders model a love of learning and a commitment to perpetually learn when they choose to read during leisure time (and talk about that practice); or perhaps they listen to audiobooks or podcasts while commuting.

Another form of learning about learning in which school leaders engage is reflective journaling. One elementary principal and his colleague, a principal at the high school, regularly spend 10 minutes, individually, at the end of the day to reflect and write. Periodically they get together to have breakfast and share their reflections in writing. Asked about this practice, one of them said, "It is a powerful way to consolidate thoughts. So much goes on, and so quickly, during any given day. Taking the time to write allows time for reflection, which often brings new insights. Besides, we are in the learning business. We have a moral responsibility to model that in word and deed."

Reflecting on History and the Moment: Implications for the Future

The power of modeling professional growth and lifelong learning is an important leverage point and tool for highly effective school leaders. Learning can happen in many contexts. Sometimes it is planned and strategically focused. Other times, it unfolds as a result of experience. Consider developing a strategic, professional development plan following a format such as the one shown on the next page.

Professional Development Plan

Name:

My Leadership Vision:

School Focus:

District Focus:

Data That Support the Focus:

After developing a professional development plan, you can then specify your professional development goals.

Professional Development Plan Goals

1. Leadership Goals (What I Intend to Achieve):

Rationale:

Indicators of Progress:

Date for Assessment of Progress:

2. Learning Goals (What I Intend to Achieve):

Rationale:

Indicators of Progress:

Date for Assessment of Progress:

Reflecting on your leadership work, use this space to jot down the contexts in which you learn and the ways in which you learn or promote learning:

How does the learning in which you engage influence others?

Use this space to jot down any other ideas, insights, or new perspectives from this chapter that you wish to add to your repertoire as a school leader:

CHAPTER TEN

Believing That Hope
Can Become a Reality

Of all the factors vital to improving schools, none is more
essential—or vulnerable—than hope.
—Robert Evans, *The Human Side of School Change*, p. 290

To help school leaders understand the change process, Evans (1996) draws
on the Lincoln experience to show how successful change occurred during
the Civil War. Evans suggests that school leaders can learn from President
Lincoln's example by maintaining *clarity and focus* (p. 222). However, Evans
warns that clarity and focus are not enough to implement successful change:
hope must also be present. Moreover, the community must recognize that
for hope to be realized, both *realism and reach* must be embraced. Evans
describes hope as a "balancing" act between realism and reach: "It means not
expanding the horizon of goals faster than dedicated people can advance"
(p. 291).

Consider how Evans's description matches Lincoln's deliberate approach
during the Civil War. Most historians agree that if Lincoln had proposed full
emancipation in 1861, he would have failed to keep the border states (Dela-
ware, Kentucky, Maryland, and Missouri) in the Union. Without the support
of the border states, the goal of preserving the Union would likely have failed.
As the war continued, Lincoln's reach toward emancipation was constantly
tested, and realism often won the day. John Hope Franklin (2009) notes,
"The Proclamation was prepared, but the propitious moment for its issu-
ance seemed never to come" (p. 198). The limited Union victory at Antietam

signaled that the "propitious moment" had arrived, and Lincoln acted. Realism and reach were joined. Hope became reality. Striner (2006) views Lincoln's political behavior as a mix of Machiavellian planning (realism) and ethical conduct (reach): "Lincoln was a rare man indeed; a fervent idealist endowed with a remarkable gift for strategy" (p. 2).

Thus, for hope to become reality, a community must have more than a vision, regardless of how just the vision is. The conditions must be assessed. Weighing context is critical: What is realistic at this time—to reach our goals? How far should we reach? Reach *and* realism must be partners. Reach is the moral component that inspires people to pursue a vision. Reach is a formidable hurdle and a primary reason why change, especially sustainable change, often is unrealized or abandoned. But reach should never be abandoned when a goal is worthwhile. Coincidentally, historian Mark Neeley makes a similar point related to realism and reach when discussing Lincoln's significant shift from negotiating with secessionist states in 1861 to supporting the Thirteenth Amendment in 1864 to abolish slavery. Neeley (2009) states that Lincoln's "ability to balance short-term practicality and long-term ideals is perhaps the essence of statesmanship" (p. 242). Hope is about pursuing ideals, but achieving short-term practical goals is the manna that provides the energy and confidence ("we can see our progress") so critical to reaching significant goals.

School goals related to social justice—such as closing the achievement gap, academic excellence for all, educating worthy citizens, pressing for gender equity, tackling the high school dropout crisis, reducing school bullying, and educating the whole child—must be pursued by school leaders because the goals, the hopes, are worthy regardless of the hurdles. On this point of principle, Evans quotes the famous playwright and eventual Czech president, Vaclav Havel:

> Hope is definitely not the same thing as optimism. It's not the conviction that something will turn out well, but the certainty that something makes sense, regardless of how it turns out. It is this hope, above all, that gives us strength to live and to continually try new things, even in conditions that seem . . . hopeless. (Havel, in Evans, 1996, p. 298)

Hope as Reflected in Lincoln's Message

On February 27, 1860, Lincoln gave an address at the Cooper Union college in New York City that is often touted as the speech that boosted his presidential chances. Essentially, Lincoln stated that the nation's founders opposed expanding slavery, recognizing that the practice was an affront to democratic principles. Thus, the present federal government (the Union) should not back down from its position because sections of the country threatened to secede. He closed the address with an idea similar to Havel's point exemplifying the essence of hope:

> Neither let us be slandered from our duty by false accusations against us, nor frightened from it by menaces of destruction to the Government . . . LET US HAVE FAITH THAT RIGHT MAKES MIGHT, AND IN THAT FAITH, LET US, TO THE END, DARE TO DO OUR DUTY AS WE UNDERSTAND IT. (Basler, 1953–1955, Vol. III, p. 550)

Lincoln's Cooper Union Address underscored the importance of moral principle, a critical component if hope is to become a reality. "Let us have faith that right makes might" implies that if you have faith (hope) in an idea, your belief can lift up your spirits, providing the capacity and desire to fight and succeed. As we have mentioned previously, the Emancipation Proclamation—and its natural consequence, the freeing of all slaves—added a moral component with national and international implications. Recall Lincoln's words in Chapter 2 from the August 1863 Conkling letter; his words are almost prophetic:

> It will then have been proved that, among free men, there can be no successful appeal from the ballot to the bullet; and that they who take such appeal are sure to lose their case, and pay the cost. And then, there will be some black men who can remember that, with silent tongue, and clenched teeth, and steady eye, and well-poised bayonet, they have helped mankind on to this great consummation; while, I fear, there will be some white ones, unable to forget that, with malignant heart, and deceitful speech, they have strove to hinder it. (Basler, 1953–1955, Vol. VI, pp. 409–410)

Again, this is not language that Lincoln could have used in 1861 to mobilize the North. Realism trumped reach, regardless of Lincoln's hope for the nation.

The Importance of the Moment: How Context Transformed Lincoln

A hope, a belief, a faith in an idea can inspire citizens or a community to engage in work that can last a lifetime. Most historians agree that Lincoln experienced a political transformation and became inspired to act when the Kansas-Nebraska law passed in Congress in 1854, increasing the possibility that slavery would expand into new states. Burlingame (2008) describes the "new" Lincoln following the Kansas-Nebraska Act: "Like a butterfly hatching from a caterpillar's chrysalis, the partisan warrior of the 1830s and 1840s was transformed into a statesman" (Vol. 1, p. 376). Lincoln's new message of hope was now for mankind, not just the United States. Lincoln expressed this in his October 16, 1854, "Peoria Speech." In the following section Lincoln is talking about the spread of slavery:

> I hate it because of the monstrous injustice of slavery itself. I hate it because it deprives our republican example of its just influence in the world—enables the enemies of free institutions, with plausibility, to taunt us as hypocrites—causes the real friends of freedom to doubt our sincerity, and especially because it forces so many really good men amongst ourselves into an open war with the very fundamental principles of civil liberty—criticizing the Declaration of Independence. (Basler, 1953–1955, Vol. II, p. 255)

Later in the speech Lincoln again invokes the Declaration of Independence and states, "No man is good enough to govern another man, *without that other's consent*" (p. 266, emphasis in original); and toward the end of the address he affirms, "Slavery is founded in the selfishness of man's nature—opposition to it, in his love of justice" (p. 271). No one who heard the words of Lincoln in Peoria, or read the speech during the following days, could miss his point: your position on the issue of slavery is not just about a state's right to set its own laws, or about economics; your position describes where you stand on the higher moral laws invoked in the Declaration of Independence. The Declaration states, "We hold these truths to be self-evident: that all men are created equal; that they are endowed by their Creator with certain inalienable rights; that among these are life, liberty, and the pursuit of happiness."

Lincoln's reverence for the Declaration is a fundamental thread found in his work. To actually hope for success in a democratic society free of despotism, where people could determine their future and realize their dreams, was, in Lincoln's world, a "promise" of the Declaration. Certainly his own experience—an example of hope realized—proved the truth of the fundamental proposition, *all men are created equal.*

From Peoria to Gettysburg, Lincoln never wavered from the message of hope promised in the Declaration of Independence. The message of hope still echoes from Gettysburg:

> It is rather for us to be here dedicated to the great task remaining before us . . . that these dead shall not have died in vain—that this nation, under God, shall have a new birth of freedom—and that government of the people, by the people, for the people, shall not perish from the earth.

An interesting interpretation of the "new birth of freedom" is that it is not only about a world of emancipation for black slaves, it is also about ending autocratic government worldwide. At the time of the American Civil War, there were several democratic national movements throughout the world in different stages of development. Some of Lincoln's supporters stressed this point and believed that the Gettysburg speech reflected the president's broader international position. Recall Lincoln's annual message to Congress on December 1, 1862: "We cannot escape history. . . . We say we are for the Union. The world will not forget that we say this." Lincoln is suggesting in 1862, and again at Gettysburg, that the hope of the democratic world, to some extent, will depend on whether the American experiment succeeds. Today, some consider Lincoln's language jingoistic. But when engaging in historical analysis it is important to ask: What was Lincoln's vision, based on the world he knew? When one considers Lincoln's origins, limited formal education, and limited travels, we are again reminded of his capacity for growth. For him to take such a worldview at Gettysburg regarding the implications of the American Civil War reminds us, again, of the moral stakes that Lincoln believed were at risk. For him, the hope of a democratic world was the goal.

Expressing Hope with Conviction and Simplicity

School leaders often reflect on questions related to hope: To make a difference, where do I begin my quest? How can I bring hope to our students, their families, our school, and our community? Engaging in work that inspires others to hope for a better world is courageous work. Effectively articulating questions and messages of hope with simplicity, and inspiring others with that message, is a skill that must be practiced. Again, Lincoln's example should be studied. He communicated a message of hope to citizens whose very lives depended on their willingness to accept the message. This was a sacred, daunting, and humbling responsibility. Lincoln carried out that responsibility with conviction and simple, clear language. Consider Lincoln's remarks to a regiment of Ohio soldiers returning from war on August 23, 1864:

> I suppose you are going home to see your families and friends. For the service you have done in this great struggle in which we are engaged I present you sincere thanks for myself and the country. I almost always feel inclined, when I happen to say anything to soldiers, to impress upon them in a few brief remarks the importance of success in this contest. It is not merely for today, but for all time to come that we should perpetuate for our children's children this great and free government, which we have enjoyed all of our lives. I beg you to remember this, not merely for my sake, but for yours. . . . It is in order that each of you may have through this free government which we have enjoyed, an open field and a fair chance for your industry, enterprise and intelligence; that you may all have equal privileges in the race of life, with all its desirable human aspirations. It is for this the struggle should be maintained, that we may not lose our birthright. The nation is worth fighting for, to secure such an inestimable jewel. (Basler, 1953–1955, Vol. VII, p. 512)

Here Lincoln describes the birthright of freedom as a "jewel." All of the soldiers could "see" the vision he was describing. The jewel is the opportunity to pursue one's aspirations supported by a free government. Without driving the point too hard, Lincoln makes a distinction between a despotic nation in which common people toil for others and give up personal dreams, and the possibilities of a free government in which personal hopes are realized. (Lincoln knows that his points should be made "in a few brief remarks"; after all, the Ohio soldiers wanted to go home!)

An Incalculable Variable: The Stature of the Messenger

Although hope includes a meaningful dream, thoughtful short-term and long-term strategies, articulation of a message, and operating as a team, other dynamics must be present. One such dynamic is the belief in the individual or individuals who lead the effort. We make judgments about taking "journeys of hope" based on the character and personality of the leaders. Do we respect and trust the leadership? Do we believe in their character? Leaders are real people, not abstractions; they have personalities.

In Chapter 4 we examined the personal example that Lincoln set for the nation; here we specifically discuss his example as it relates to hope. After Lincoln was martyred, his personal flaws and political mistakes were often overlooked. To forget that he was flawed and recognize only the "better angels" would be an unfortunate assessment, one that ignores his own human struggles and capacity for growth. McGovern (2009) notes that biography reminds us that presidents also have failings and that Lincoln "could be moody and sullen, stubborn and insensitive, [and, at times,] his melancholy took over" (p. 13). McGovern stresses that we "do not want perfect heroes . . . [we prefer] individuals who can overcome their inadequacies and accomplish great things" (p. 13).

When examining how Lincoln was viewed during the Civil War, we find countless examples of individuals who saw him as flawed, who saw the failings but were willing to stick with him because of a belief in his character and the general direction he was taking the nation. Harriet Beecher Stowe had reservations about Lincoln's ability to move quickly on important issues and about how his actions "troubled" many. Yet Stowe stated, "It was never that we doubted the goodwill of our pilot—only the clearness of his eyesight" (Stowe in Holzer, 2009, p. 180). Abolitionist Lydia Maria Child, often very critical of Lincoln, stated in 1864, "I have sometimes been out of patience with him; but I will say of him that I have constantly gone on liking him better and better" (Child in Burlingame, 2008, Vol. 2, p. 728). The comments of Stowe and Child are similar to observations by abolitionist Frederick Douglass and newspaper editor Horace Greeley mentioned in earlier chapters of this book. All slowly learned to respect and trust the character of the leader. They came to believe that the nation's hopes could become a reality with Lincoln at the helm. This same message holds weight for today; faith in the character of the leadership is a critical dynamic if a community hopes to accomplish its goals. A journey of hope starts with character.

President Barack Obama, in *The Audacity of Hope* (2006), discusses the significance of Lincoln's character as an inspirational source. Obama begins by noting Lincoln's "humanity" and "imperfections," and then states, "His capacity to overcome personal loss and remain determined in the face of repeated defeat—in all of this, we see a fundamental element of the American character, a belief that we can constantly remake ourselves *to fit our larger dreams*" (p. 122, emphasis added). Obama's phrase "to fit our larger dreams" is another way of expressing hope. We must first dream it; a vision must be crystallized before it can be developed and implemented. Lincoln's character and own struggles—his personal story—embodied the national dream. Today's leaders must be willing to share their stories so community members know where the passion for hope began.

Lincoln's Life and Work: Implications for School Leaders

Much of this chapter so far has addressed how intangibles—clarity, focus, hope, moral purpose, even imperfections—contributed to realizing a grand vision of democracy for a nation. Leaders must model these same intangibles in the real work that they do, day in and day out, to help all members of the organization thrive. But how can leaders model something like hope and perseverance in the face of adversity, to achieve success? Richard Sagor (2009) offers food for thought:

> We know the facts. Nearly 50 percent of Latino, black, and American Indian youth leave school before graduating (Orfield, Losen, Wald, &

Swanson, 2004). The academic performance of students in low-income communities lags well behind that of students living in more privileged enclaves. The message most often taken from movies like *Stand and Deliver* [or *Freedom Writers*] is that these students' success was the result of the magical powers of a few special, charismatic teachers.

Hollywood wants us to think that Escalante and Gruwell [the star teachers portrayed in *Stand and Deliver* and *Freedom Writers*, respectively] are superheroes, but I'd rather think of them as colleagues who have demonstrated an important lesson regarding what it takes to motivate all our diverse students to strive for the best. (pp. 45–46)

Sagor continues by suggesting that the content of the "important lesson" demonstrated by teacher leaders involves optimism. Optimism requires a positive belief in the future. And, he claims, it can be taught and learned. Sagor explains there are two key variables, *faith* and *efficacy*, that represent the building blocks of optimism. Regarding faith, Sagor states the following:

For me to invest time and energy today for a benefit I won't realize until tomorrow, I need to have a good reason to believe that my investment will pay off. Clearly, it's much easier to acquire that faith when one's immediate environment regularly shows concrete evidence of return on investment. . . . If children see despair around them, it's likely that they will fear that this represents their destiny. . . . If the picture is rosier, however, children have a better chance of being optimistic about their futures.

To affirm his point about faith, Sagor shares the story of philanthropist Eugene Lang, who started the "I Have a Dream" Foundation. Lang once promised 61 New York public school students (6th graders) a college education if they remained in school until graduating. Lang's promise inspired 90 percent of the students to graduate; two-thirds attended college. These statistics contrasted with the expectation that 75 percent of these students would *not* graduate from high school (White, 1987). Faith in the possibility of a brighter future made a difference.

Commenting on the second key variable, Sagor states that efficacy entails a major commitment beyond faith:

> Optimistic people have the fortitude to persevere with complex tasks because they are confident that if they work long and hard enough and apply enough creativity, they will, in fact, succeed. Efficacy is a deep-seated belief in our own capabilities. It explains the phenomenon of success breeding success. Every time people attack a problem and succeed, they have authentic evidence of their capability. The more data I have about my capabilities, the more confident I will be of my potential to achieve future success. (p. 48)

Sagor illustrates how these two building blocks—faith and efficacy—work together to change schools by telling a story. An English teacher and a doctoral student in a Southern California middle school that served a racially and economically diverse community invited interested students to join them in an investigation of "obstacles" to school learning (in SooHoo, 1993). Twelve students met during lunchtime for regular discussions. These student researchers, including English language learners, were mostly immigrants and minority students. They used cameras and sketchpads to record data. After several months they presented ideas for program improvement. They "had ideas about changing the school's discipline and reward policy as well as the physical education program" (Sagor, 2009, p. 51) but realized they did not have the power to bring about the desired changes. The students and their adult mentors requested and were granted an opportunity to present their research at a faculty meeting, which they also catered, bringing snacks. Later, during a professional development day, the students worked with the middle school teachers to revise the discipline and reward process and redesigned the physical education program for the following year. This experience created within these students a belief that they could, and would, achieve their goals. Every one of them was "certain they were headed to college and professional careers" (p. 52).

Of course, not all stories have such delightful endings. But Sagor's insightful message about reaching an "achievable dream" cannot be missed: encouragement, hope, and authentic stories and examples of success must be emphasized by teachers each day if students are to believe in a better future. In these examples, a theme of collaboration echoes through the stories—collaboration that involves teacher leaders, students, and administrators, driven by a moral purpose. And the work they do affects not only the experience these players have today, but also the life and career paths of tomorrow for every individual. Fueled by a sense of optimism, strengthened by faith and efficacy, their dreams can and will be realized.

Instructional resources and a building do not make a school. People—students, teachers, and parents—make a school. At night, when the doors close, it is an empty shell. And students are the soul of the school. Students come to our schools with diverse experiences, needs, learning challenges, and preferences for learning. The intent is that each student will achieve both excellence and equality. In *The Principal's Companion* (Robbins & Alvy, 2009), we define the quest for excellence and equality as part of the democratic ideal, and as a social justice imperative:

> As we move further away from ability grouping and traditional high school tracking, provide the least restrictive environment for children with disabilities, [address gender bias], and successfully meet the needs of students from diverse backgrounds, our democratic ideals can become a classroom reality. Many nations track students early for high schools, colleges, and careers; in this context, the "late bloomer" would not have a chance to reach his or her potential. Reaching for excellence and equality is a tall order, but it is a noble goal [that every nation should] seek to attain. Today, this quest for excellence and equality has become an important moral issue for school [leaders] in general, under the phrase *social justice*. (p. 194)

It is important to note that the *Educational Leadership Policy Standards: ISLLC 2008* address social justice as an important duty of the principalship. Standard 5 is related to integrity, fairness, and ethical leadership; concerning social justice, the standard includes the following principalship function: "Promote social justice and ensure that individual student needs inform all aspects of schooling." To help school leaders gain a better understanding of social justice responsibilities, McKenzie and colleagues (2008) define three social justice goals, all with a moral purpose:

> Rais[ing] the academic achievement of all students in their school, that is, test scores do matter . . . although we advocate for a variety of measures of student learning and are well aware of the problems associated

with standardized achievement tests, we contend that they still have a place in the social justice discourse.

> Requir[ing] that educational leaders for social justice prepare their students to live as critical citizens in society . . . [who] challenge injustices in society.

> Requir[ing] leaders to structure their schools to ensure that students learn in heterogeneous, inclusive classrooms. (p. 116)

These social justice goals raise the stakes for school leaders and help us to recognize that equality and excellence are both worthy goals. It is not an either/or dilemma. Should we emphasize high-stakes testing that may pressure some students to drop out, or try to keep students in school by providing the necessary social support? Social justice leaders know that success on high-stakes tests is important, but that realization does not mean ignoring multiple and formative assessment measures that can help students do better on high-stakes tests *and* provide rich data to help teachers meet individual student needs. Leaders need to do whatever it takes to ensure that every student excels.

It has been said that just as what you do is important, how you do it is equally, if not more, important. As school leaders pursue those strategic actions that will ensure that their vision, driven by a moral purpose, is realized, they must ponder the following questions:

- What will I do to engender trust in me as a leader among organizational members?
- How might I earn the respect of those in the school and larger community?
- How will I become comfortable in allowing my imperfections to show, so that others will see me as approachable and will feel comfortable allowing their frailties to show?

Earlier in the chapter, we discussed Lincoln's humanity and imperfections. The flaws for which he was known made him human and real; and they provided a profound message that a common man could accomplish extraordinary things. Similarly, Judith Warren Little (1982), a noted professor at the University of California, Berkeley, once advised a group of school leaders in Napa, California, "It's important to let your rough edges show. They give you something to hold onto to examine your practice. So I encourage rough edges." A high school principal was so moved by this advice that she handed out rough stones at the next faculty meeting and shared Judith Warren Little's quote. She invited teacher colleagues to keep their stones on their desks and use them as a source of reflection. She said, "As you gaze upon your stone, reflect upon your practices and what you might do to refine them—as if you are polishing the stone." As a celebration of their efforts, at the end-of-the-year faculty meeting, the principal leadership team showed a DVD of four student testimonials. These featured students from the high school who, at the beginning of the year, were failing their courses, but because of teachers' efforts were achieving at high levels at the end of the year. After the DVD concluded, many staff members had tears in their eyes. The leadership team concluded the meeting by saying, "As ordinary people, you do extraordinary things to make a difference for students, and our tomorrow. We thank you."

Reflecting on History and the Moment:
Implications for the Future

This chapter focused on hope as an element of change. Ponder how hope can be a part of your transformational work as a leader and record your thoughts in the space below.

The message of hope for the future still echoes from Gettysburg: *"It is rather for us to be here dedicated to the great task remaining before us."* As school leaders we face so many inequalities in the world—the growing homeless population, inadequate human and material resources for English language learners, needs for students from poverty who are without privilege, addressing diverse and non-"mainstream" cultures, students who come to schools from warring nations—the list goes on. To what will you "be here dedicated"? Use this space to record your thoughts.

- What is the "great task remaining"?

Our actions as school leaders influence the optimism and hope we offer our students. At the end of each day ponder the following questions:

- As a result of each student's experience in school today, how will his or her life be better?
- What have we done as educators to help students perceive that their futures are bright?

If we can positively address these questions with specific examples, we will have contributed to improving our schools, families, communities, nation, and humankind.

Use this space to jot down any other ideas, insights, or new perspectives from this chapter that you wish to add to your repertoire as a school leader.

CHAPTER ELEVEN

Achieving Authentic Leadership in Schools

Upon the subject of education, not presuming to dictate any plan or system respecting it, I can only say that I view it as the most important subject which we as a people can be engaged in.
—From Abraham Lincoln's first campaign announcement
for the Illinois state legislature, March 9, 1832

In this last chapter it is important to revisit the introductory question that we promised to address in this book: What can educational leaders learn from an in-depth study of Lincoln's leadership experiences to achieve success in today's schools? To answer this question we have examined Lincoln's enduring legacy and have applied it to our 21st century leadership responsibilities. Reflecting on the legacy, consider the opening quote of this chapter. Without receiving a formal education himself, Lincoln declared, at the age of 23, that education was essential for a people to succeed. He admitted that it would be presumptuous to "dictate any plan" of education, yet, as we have noted throughout this book, Lincoln's example demonstrates the power of self-education. His capacity for growth through self-education, and continued growth as an individual and a leader, might be the greatest lesson today's educational leaders can gain from Lincoln's story. Those of us who work with adults who must constantly improve their craft, both individually and as team members, to make a difference for all children, cannot ignore the inspirational personal example and leadership modeling that Lincoln provided for us. Interestingly, historian Michael Burlingame (2009) makes a similar point: "As I conduct research about [Lincoln] and write about him, I feel compelled to try to be a better historian and a better human being. I try and will continue to try" (p. 4).

Examining Lincoln's mistakes and how he grew from his miscalculations is also an essential aspect of the story that contemporary leaders need to heed when assessing their own crisis-and-response behavior. Lincoln had flaws; he erred, but learned. James Horton (2009) states it this way:

> In this age, when some charge any revision of political position as a "flip flop" and consider thoughtless consistency a praiseworthy political attribute, we would do well to remember one of the most important political figures in American history, President Abraham Lincoln, a man who learned from personal experience and changed his mind. (p. 63)

Thus, as we review and try to synthesize Lincoln's significant leadership qualities, we must remember that the capacity to grow, which we focused on as a leadership quality in Chapter 9, is the thread that connects and unites the other leadership attributes. When Frederick Douglass told Lincoln that the Second Inaugural Address was a "sacred effort," he was referring not only to the speech but also to how far Lincoln had traveled, in terms of revising his views, concerning the proposition that "all men are created equal." Douglass knew that he had influenced the president and that Lincoln's views had progressed in some measure because of the performance of the black troops and their contribution to preserving the Union and ending slavery (Horton, 2009). Let us not forget that a moment before Douglass's "sacred effort" comment, Lincoln had asked for Douglass's view by stating, "There is no man in the country whose opinion I value more than yours."

To assess the 21st century implication of Lincoln's leadership qualities, it is important to restate the attributes and skills discussed in the 10 previous chapters. As you review the 10 qualities, keep in mind that for Lincoln to succeed, each quality was needed, and the interrelated whole (the 10 qualities together) is what led to his success. Consider how this reality could apply to a 21st century school leader. For example, if one is to accomplish a mission, then tenacity and persistence become critical personal attributes needed to survive through the difficult times when one could easily waver, give up, and abandon the mission. The 10 qualities, attributes, and skills are as follows:

1. Implementing and sustaining a mission and vision with focused and profound clarity
2. Communicating ideas effectively with precise and straightforward language
3. Building a diverse and competent team to successfully address the mission
4. Engendering trust, loyalty, and respect through humility, humor, and personal example
5. Leading and serving with emotional intelligence and empathy
6. Exercising situational competence and responding appropriately to implement effective change
7. Rising beyond personal and professional trials through tenacity, persistence, resilience, and courage
8. Exercising purposeful visibility
9. Demonstrating personal growth and enhanced competence as a lifetime learner, willing to reflect on and expand ideas
10. Believing that hope can become a reality

Implementing Lincoln's Enduring Example: A Scenario

To demonstrate how these qualities apply to our time and are related to each other, consider the following vision, a scenario of how a 21st century district and school leadership team might use Lincoln's example to address a major challenge.

In the Jefferson School District, the central office leadership team and the school leadership teams are determined to close the achievement gap among various racial and ethnic groups in the elementary, middle, and high schools. Central office and school leaders all agree that they are engaged in a moral battle to enable students to reach their highest potential and achieve their dreams in school and in the workplace. The central office and school

personnel, including teacher leaders, have been reading selected books, jour-
nals, and studies on closing the achievement gap, and they have been sharing
their ideas in formal and informal settings. Team members have also visited some exemplary schools in the state. The leaders have been particularly
impressed with studies that emphasize the following:

- Academic rigor and meeting standards
- The importance of relationships
- Immediate interventions for struggling students
- Personalization of content for all students
- Individual and group social support beyond academics, especially for
students who are at risk for dropping out
- Emphasizing individual responsibility as a critical value
- Building a culture of district and school pride
- Distributing professional, shared leadership throughout the school
- Promoting teacher development related to best and promising practices
in professional learning communities
- Working with parent and community constituencies

The district personnel are determined to succeed, are developing a
thoughtful plan, and recognize that success will not occur overnight. On the
other hand, they know that too much planning can slow down an effort; they
want to get started! The unwritten mantra of the district is "ready, fire, aim,"
learn from mistakes, and do better next time. Although the district has a mission and vision statement in place, district and school leaders have developed,
with teacher support (and the backing of the school board), a mission statement specifically for this effort. The statement is this:

> Seizing the Future Together as a Professional Community of
> Learners Through Leading and Teaching, Embracing Personal
> and Collaborative Responsibilities for Each Student's Academic,
> Social, Citizenship, and Wellness Success

Although there was eventual consensus on the project mission statement, several teacher leaders and administrators thought it was particularly

important to use the phrase "seizing the future" so their effort would not be perceived as passive about future jobs and the technological world that awaits students. Other professionals were firm about using the word "each" instead of "all" students, so students would not be perceived as a collective, with some being lost in the shuffle. Further, unless a community embraces the moral responsibility and acts on the words, a mission statement will likely become just a wall ornament. This struggle for precision in language is a testament to the individual meaning people bring to the consensus-building process. In addition, the struggle and its resolution creates the synergy to fuel the collective effort to accomplish the mission.

Central office personnel, school administrators, and teacher leaders know it is their collective responsibility to set personal examples, serving the needs of students and other teachers. The administrators are particularly pleased that the teacher leaders represent a broad range of teaching philosophies yet are on the same page concerning the mission. The superintendent is pleased, also, that her decision to hire a combination of newcomer and veteran administrators the past few years seems to be paying off. Some of those hired are from inside the district, whereas others were hired from outside. The combination seems to work, as district insiders raise issues about possible school culture "traps," while the outsiders push for taking risks and shaking up the culture.

To share the goals of the mission and to address the importance of reducing the achievement gap, the leadership teams are developing strategies to communicate to each segment of the community. Leaders are determined to avoid educational jargon with students, parents, guardians, and the greater community. Additionally, the administrators and teachers are specifically reviewing intervention strategies with students and are engaging in group and individual meetings with parents and guardians to review what can be done at home to support the schools' efforts. Volunteer translators from the schools and community, including parents, student graduates, and present students, are used to ensure the message is being relayed to everyone.

An interesting strategy used in a coordinated manner by the administration and teacher leadership teams during meetings with teachers, parents, and students is to realistically assess what has worked and has not worked. This honest approach is possible because the leaders have done their homework on the research related to achievement, especially concerning diverse groups that were unsuccessful in the past because of inadequate programs. Students who are representative of the student population at the schools are also being consulted, because leadership teams value their perspective. Although some who are engaging in this discussion are uneasy with the dialogue, the rationale for the approach is sound: this is hard work, teaching is a highly sophisticated science and art, our society and institutions often fail, funding is often inadequate, and students are very complex.

The discussions with some groups and individuals become heated at times. Various topics percolate during the discussions generated by the achievement-gap issues, including inadequate funding for the district and individual schools, questionable budgetary priorities, teacher dedication, parental commitment, student laziness, too many instructional fads, and too few funds for professional development. Also discussed are racism, bullying, a lack of focus concerning academically talented students, inadequate progress for special education and English language learners, too much or not enough testing, the quality of textbooks, time allocated for shared planning and problem solving, and technology needs. Yet, at the end of each meeting, almost everyone has agreed that the present effort to close the achievement gap is important. The community appreciates the patient listening of the administration and teacher leaders, and the sincere empathy and respect for the various constituencies. The leaders even use humor or an appropriate story with teachers, parents, or student groups to reduce the tension generated by some issues or to make a salient point.

Although this is a recently launched initiative, the leaders have all experienced previous successful and unsuccessful change efforts. Each knows that context is critical and there will be disappointments along the way. The leaders are well aware that change is difficult and that most individuals do not embrace change, regardless of public statements to the contrary. Personal meaning must be part of the process. Key personnel ask questions such as these: Will this make a difference for me? Will I be a more effective teacher as a result of the effort? Will I be a more effective administrator? Will this really help to close the achievement gap? The administrators and teacher leaders know that they will have to persist during the difficult days when it looks like they are going backward—or at least not moving forward. (Some may look for an easy way out, possibly suggesting that they try something else, something new.) However, the leadership is determined to keep the eye on the ball. They know that the work is a "calling." Every student is entitled to reach his or her potential; it is one's birthright.

As the program develops, the district and school leadership teams are determined to monitor progress and review data. They will follow conventional and unconventional strategies. Data based on summative test results will be reviewed, and teachers will be expected to engage in formative assessments to review student progress over time and to intervene immediately when the data indicate that a specific student is not thriving. In professional learning communities, teachers will work on formative, common assessments with colleagues. To support their efforts, administrators from the district and the schools will visit classrooms—Leading and Learning By Wandering Around, as described in Chapter 8—primarily to celebrate successes and provide immediate positive feedback to teachers about their strategies. Teacher leaders will also be engaged in the LLBWA process. All teachers will be encouraged to visit classrooms of colleagues and share best and promising practices. Moreover, spreading the word about successful practices will be encouraged, not only among grade-level or department teams, but also across schools in the district. Thus, lateral capacity building will be emphasized (Fullan, 2007). Sharing successful strategies in professional development settings within the professional learning community will be a cornerstone of the effort to fulfill the mission. Sensitive to individual needs, the administrators recognize that each school and classroom will modify best and promising strategies to meet contextual differences, including addressing individual, class, and school needs. Thus, the grand design of the mission can be implemented only when the unique nuts-and-bolts needs of each classroom are addressed.

The administration and teacher leaders, because of their own experiences related to exciting moments of growth with new ideas, recognize the importance of constantly learning. Thus, promoting the essential elements of professional learning communities among administrators and teachers will be an essential cultural goal within and across the district. A theme of lifelong learning will, ideally, become embedded in the fabric of each school. Administrators and teacher leaders also will be encouraged to communicate the importance of their own learning experiences not only to other administrators and teachers, but also to students. Students are often surprised to learn that their teachers and principals are still going to school, but hearing the message that learning never ends and that we all need to get better at what we do must be communicated to students and embedded in school culture.

Sharing and celebrating successes must be part of the culture of the Jefferson School District. Doing so provides the hope and inspiration to continue the journey to accomplish the mission. Thus the district has developed a plan to invite successful alumni and parents to school events, such as career days, to share their stories. Also, the administration and teacher leaders have developed strategies to acknowledge individual student and group successes. Contacting the media concerning successes is also built into the plan. To emphasize positive news and to build trust with families, administrators and teacher leaders are using their cell phones and the Internet proactively, to contact parents and guardians to share student successes. To keep hope alive for students who are having difficulties, immediate intervention programs are in effect. The schools recognize that hope diminishes when frustration levels increase. Consequently, teachers and administrators—with help from students, parents, and guardians—are determined to minimize this possibility of frustration and failure. Leadership teams are also sharing positive results and their strategies with various foundations to secure funding to further address needs. Some of the funding is supporting college scholarships for students, and the school guidance counselors are determined to remain in touch with the scholarship recipients so they will return during breaks to share their stories of success.

Finally, the central office and school leadership teams meet once a month to review progress and consider strategy refinements to address real-time developments indicated by both qualitative and quantitative data. The teams recognize that mistakes will be made, but they want to learn from the mistakes to make judicious but quick midcourse corrections, always keeping their eye on the mission. The superintendent recognizes that "honest stumbling along the way" is simply part of the change journey when striving to reach a worthy mission. She reminded the teams that they will be judged on results, and then shared a brief intentional point about mission with the school leaders. She quoted Frederick Douglass's words on June 1, 1865, describing how millions of black Americans felt about the death of their fallen president:

> They viewed him *not in the light of separate individual acts, but in the light of his mission,* in his manifest relation to events and in the philosophy of his statesmanship. Viewing him thus they trusted him as men are seldom trusted. (Douglass, in Burlingame, 2009, p. 4, emphasis added)

The Jefferson School District Scenario: Implications for School Leaders

The preceding scenario is about leaders making contextually thoughtful, inclusive choices, driven by a sacred vision of excellence and equality. Undoubtedly, each of you could create a scenario based on your school district and integrate the described leadership strategies into it. However, if context is critical, then one must be very careful about trying to simply plug in leadership strategies that may have worked in a different context. The intent of this book is *not* to provide a foolproof recipe for leadership success. The intent is to provide an enduring example of how one leader, Abraham Lincoln, used his unique and considerable skills to succeed, drawing upon cultivated inner resources and driven by a moral purpose to make a difference. Authentic leadership can emerge based only on what you thoughtfully and honestly bring to the table. Past experiences, the current organizational situation, and examples and ideas of others regarding successful practice will strengthen and enhance your leadership capacity.

School leaders should view the previous 10 chapters as an intellectual challenge that delves deep into the heart of leadership. We encourage you, the reader, to view the Lincoln example as a reprieve from a formulaic equation that minimizes your own strengths. Instead, view the example as a leadership story that can inspire thoughtful decision making about your own leadership behavior in today's schools. We trust that leaders will exercise intellectual rigor in making sound decisions after reading Lincoln's story. We hope that Lincoln's example will serve as an inspiration to examine your own powerful stories and will engender the thoughtfulness, insights, and energy necessary to make sound decisions.

One of the most important elements of success will be how you lead by example. If the Lincoln legacy is about personal growth, then you can use the lessons of that legacy to find the passion to pursue your own growth. Lincoln's passion included a desire to be remembered for contributing to society. However, without politics and a lifelong fervor for the intrigue of political battle, the means for making a contribution may not have emerged. School leaders are fortunate. The means for making a contribution are available each day: we have the opportunity to work with students, professional colleagues, and the community.

In the first part of the 21st century, each individual's path to leadership success will be different. We are not contemporaries of Lincoln, but, like Lincoln, we have chosen a profession that can make a difference in the lives of others and in our future. And, like Lincoln, we know that the barriers will be formidable. We will be judged on how we perform when times are toughest. Aligning words and deeds, engaging heart and mind, being trustworthy, exercising humility, and demonstrating a relentless love of learning will be key. And because our work is noble, we must persevere, keeping in mind the words of the late senator Edward Kennedy: "The fundamental test of our society is how we treat the least powerful among us." We wish you well on this most remarkable, important, and honorable journey.

Reflecting on History and the Moment: Implications for the Future

The following questions provide a structure for organizing your reflections about Lincoln's example and how it applies to the challenges of educational leadership in the 21st century. Use the space following each question to record your responses.

- What new insights about leadership have you gained as a result of Lincoln's example?

- How will you incorporate these into your repertoire of strategic leadership skills?

- As leaders, we are constantly pursuing a quest to create an inner drive within students and adults to continue learning for a lifetime. What new ideas do you have about this leadership responsibility?

- The demands for skillfulness in leadership have never been greater. This challenge has implications for both personal and professional growth. To what do you commit as a leader regarding your own growth?

- Demands for leadership action are much too complex for a single individual. What will you do to harness the collective expertise of staff to build a high-functioning leadership team that treasures the value of multiple perspectives to enhance the leadership vision and mission, and create the vitality to pursue it?

The following table lists the 10 leadership qualities, characteristics, and attributes for which Lincoln is known. We invite you to select one of the following activities that has personal meaning for you:

- Examine the list and prioritize the qualities according to your leadership beliefs and values and personal and professional needs.
- Use the list of 10 qualities as a tool to self-assess your leadership practices.

10 Qualities for Success in 21st Century Leadership	
Leadership Quality	**Indicators of Mastery, Success**
1. Implementing and sustaining a mission and vision with focused and profound clarity	
2. Communicating ideas effectively with precise and straightforward language	
3. Building a diverse and competent team to successfully address the mission	
4. Engendering trust, loyalty, and respect through humility, humor, and personal example	
5. Leading and serving with emotional intelligence and empathy	
6. Exercising situational competence and responding appropriately to implement effective change	
7. Rising beyond personal and professional trials through tenacity, persistence, resilience, and courage	
8. Exercising purposeful visibility	
9. Demonstrating personal growth and enhanced competence as a lifetime learner, willing to reflect on and expand ideas	
10. Believing that hope can become a reality	

The leader's role continues to be multifaceted and challenging. We hope that Lincoln's legacy will leave an enduring mark on your leadership practices and provide the energy, tenacity, and vitality for you to make a difference.

Abraham Lincoln reads to Tad (Thomas), one of four sons born to the
President and Mrs. (Mary Todd) Lincoln (in birth order: Robert, Edward, William, and Thomas).
Robert Todd Lincoln (1843-1926) was the only child to survive into adulthood.

APPENDIX A

A Chronology of Abraham Lincoln's Life

1809 Born near Nolin Creek in Hardin County, Kentucky, on February 12.

1816 Family moves to Indiana, possibly because it was not a slave state.

1818 Mother, Nancy Hanks Lincoln, dies, likely of "milk sickness."

1819 Father, Thomas Lincoln, marries Sarah Bush Johnson.

1824 By age 15, formal education ended; schooling totaled approximately one year.

1828 Takes a flatboat trip to New Orleans and witnesses slave auctions.

1831 Moves to New Salem, Illinois, to strike out on his own; during the next few years he splits rails, works as a postmaster, surveyor, general store clerk, and later store owner (goes bankrupt).

1832 Serves as a captain in the Black Hawk War but sees no action; runs for Illinois state legislature and loses.

1834 Begins to study law; wins first of four consecutive elections to the Illinois state legislature.

1837 Moves to Springfield and becomes a junior law partner.

1839 Travels the Eighth Circuit in Illinois as a lawyer; meets Mary Todd in Springfield.

1842 Marries Mary Todd.

1844 Sets up legal practice with William Herndon, who remains his partner until Lincoln becomes president.

1846 Is elected to the U.S. House of Representatives from Illinois, taking his seat in December of the following year.

1847   Questions President Polk's policies on the origins of the war with Mexico.

1849   Finishes congressional term and returns to his Springfield law practice.

1854   Kansas-Nebraska Act passed in Congress, likely resulting in the expansion of slavery; leads to Peoria Speech.

1856   Lincoln, a Whig, helps to organize the new Republican Party in Illinois.

1858   Is nominated as the Republican candidate for U.S. senator and gives "House Divided" speech; engages in seven famous debates with Stephen Douglas; loses the Senate election, although Republicans receive a plurality of popular votes.

1860   Gives "Right Makes Might" speech at Cooper Union in New York City; in Chicago, is nominated by Republican Party as presidential candidate; is elected president on November 6; South Carolina secedes.

1861   Gives "Springfield Farewell" Address on February 11; six more Southern states secede; delivers First Inaugural Address on March 4; Civil War begins at Ft. Sumter on April 12; suspension of habeas corpus in some areas; First Battle of Bull Run; appoints McClellan commander of the Union Army.

1862   Son Willie dies in the White House; preliminary Emancipation Proclamation is issued on September 22 following limited Antietam victory.

1863   Emancipation Proclamation becomes law on January 1; early July victories at Gettysburg and Vicksburg; delivers Gettysburg Address on November 19.

1864   In March, appoints Grant commander of the Union Army; Sherman burns Atlanta and marches to the sea; Lincoln defeats McClellan in presidential election on November 8.

1865   Congress passes Thirteenth Amendment abolishing slavery; Second Inaugural is delivered on March 4; Lee surrenders at Appomattox on April 9; Lincoln shot on April 14 and dies at 7:22 a.m. on April 15; Stanton states, "Now he belongs to the ages."

References

Ackerman, R., & Maslin-Ostrowski, P. (2004, April). The wounded leader. *Educational Leadership, 61*(7), 28–32.

Alvy, H., & Robbins, P. (1998). *If I only knew. . . : Success strategies for navigating the principalship.* Thousand Oaks, CA: Corwin Press.

Alvy, H., & Robbins, P. (2009, March). *Supporting new principals: Leadership strategies to achieve excellence.* Presentation at the ASCD Annual Conference, Orlando, FL.

Ayres, A. (1992). *The wit and wisdom of Abraham Lincoln: An A–Z compendium of quotes from the most eloquent of American presidents.* New York: Meridian Books.

Basler, R. (Ed.). (1953–1955). *The collected works of Abraham Lincoln* (Vols. I–IX). New Brunswick, NJ: Rutgers University Press.

Bennis, W. (1984). Transformative power and leadership. In T. Sergiovanni & J. Corbally (Eds.), *Leadership and organizational culture* (pp. 64–71). Urbana, IL: University of Illinois Press.

Bennis, W., & Nanus, B. (1985). *Leaders.* New York: Harper and Row.

Bryk, A., & Schneider, B. (2003, March). Trust in schools: A core resource for school reform. *Educational Leadership, 60*(6), 40–44.

Burlingame, M. (2008). *Abraham Lincoln: A life* (Vols. 1–2). Baltimore, MD: Johns Hopkins University Press.

Burlingame, M. (2009, Fall). Michael Burlingame speaks at bicentennial dinner. *For the People* (A Newsletter of the Abraham Lincoln Association), *2*(3), 3–4.

Burns, J. (1978). *Leadership.* New York: Harper and Row.

Carwardine, R. (2006). *Lincoln: A life of purpose and power.* New York: Vantage Books.

Carwardine, R. (2008). Lincoln's religion. In E. Foner (Ed.), *Our Lincoln: New perspectives on Lincoln and his world* (pp. 223–248). New York: W. W. Norton.

Clinton, C. (2008). Abraham Lincoln: The family that made him, the family he made. In E. Foner (Ed.), *Our Lincoln: New perspectives on Lincoln and his world* (pp. 249–266). New York: W. W. Norton.

Cohen, E. (2002). *Supreme command: Soldiers, statesmen, and leadership in wartime.* New York: Free Press.

Collins, J. (2001). *Good to great.* New York: Harper Business.

Collins, J. (2005). *Good to great and the social sectors.* Boulder, CO: Jim Collins.

Collins, J. (2005, May). Collins on leadership: Level 5 leadership. *TEC Leadership Notes, 2*(5). Retrieved October 4, 2009, from www.seattletec.com/enotes.may05.htm

Conger, J. (1989). *The charismatic leader: Behind the mystique of exceptional leadership.* San Francisco: Jossey-Bass.

Cotton, K. (2003). *Principals and student achievement.* Alexandria, VA: ASCD.

Crow, T. (2008, Summer). Declaration of interdependence: Educators need deep conversations about teaching and learning to spark real changes in practice (Q & A with Judith Warren Little). *Journal of Staff Development, 29*(3), 53–56.

Cuddy, A. (2009, February). Just because I'm nice don't assume I'm dumb. *Harvard Business Review, 87*(2), 24. Retrieved October 5, 2009, from hbr.org

Donald, D. (1995). *Lincoln.* New York: Simon and Schuster Paperbacks.

Donald, D. (2003). *We are Lincoln men: Abraham Lincoln and his friends.* New York: Simon and Schuster.

DuFour, R. (2001, Winter). In the right context. *Journal of Staff Development, 22*(1), 14–17.

DuFour, R., & Eaker, R. (1998). *Professional learning communities at work: Best practices for enhancing student achievement.* Bloomington, IN: National Educational Services.

Educational leadership policy standards: ISLLC 2008. (2008). Washington, DC: Council of Chief State School Officers.

Ellis, J. (2007). *American creation: Triumphs and tragedies at the founding of the republic.* New York: Alfred A. Knopf.

Evans, R. (1996). *The human side of school change.* San Francisco: Jossey-Bass.

Fehrenbacher, D. (2009). The origins and purpose of Lincoln's "house divided" speech. In S. Wilentz (Ed.), *The best American history essays on Lincoln* (pp. 149–173). New York: Palgrave Macmillan.

Ferguson, A. (2007). *Land of Lincoln.* New York: Atlantic Monthly Press.

Franklin, J. H. (1985). The use and misuse of the Lincoln legacy. *Journal of the Abraham Lincoln Association, 7*(1). Retrieved June 30, 2009, from http://www.historycooperative.org/cgi-bin/printpage.cgi

Franklin, J. H. (2009). The Emancipation Proclamation: The decision and the writing. In S. Wilentz (Ed.), *The best American history essays on Lincoln* (pp. 191–205). New York: Palgrave Macmillan.

Fullan, M. (2007). *The new meaning of educational change* (4th ed.). New York: Teachers College Press.

Gardner, H. (1995). *Leading minds: An anatomy of leadership.* New York: Basic Books.

George, B. (2007). *True north.* San Francisco: Jossey-Bass.

Glickman, C., Gordon, S., & Ross-Gordon, J. (2010). *Supervision and instructional leadership* (8th ed.). Boston: Allyn & Bacon.

Goleman, D. (1995). *Emotional intelligence.* New York: Bantam Books.

Goleman, D. (1998). *Working with emotional intelligence.* New York: Bantam Books.

Goleman, D. (1998, November–December). What makes a leader? *Harvard Business Review, 76*(6) 92–102.

Goleman, D. (2006, September). The socially intelligent leader. *Educational Leadership, 64*(1), 76–81.

Goleman, D., Boyatzis, R., &, McKee, A. (2002). *Primal leadership.* Boston: Harvard Business School Press.

Goodwin, D. K. (2005). *Team of rivals.* New York: Simon and Schuster.

Griessman, G. (1997). *The words Lincoln lived by.* New York: Fireside Books.

Heifetz, R., & Linsky, M. (2002). *Leadership on the line.* Boston: Harvard Business School Press.

Heifetz, R., & Linsky, M. (2004, April). When leadership spells danger. *Educational Leadership, 61*(7), 33–37.

Herndon, W. (1889/1970). *Herndon's Lincoln: The true story of a great life.* Indianapolis: Bobbs-Merrill.

Holzer, H. (2000). *Abraham Lincoln the writer: A treasury of his greatest speeches and letters.* Honesdale, PA: Boyds Mills Press.

Holzer, H. (2004). *Lincoln at Cooper Union.* New York: Simon and Schuster.

Holzer, H. (2009). *Lincoln as I knew him: Gossip, tributes & revelations from his best friends & worst enemies.* Chapel Hill, NC: Algonquin Paperbacks.

Horton, J. (2009). Naturally anti-slavery: Lincoln, race, and the complexity of American liberty. In S. Wilentz (Ed.), *The best American history essays on Lincoln* (pp. 63–84). New York: Palgrave Macmillan.

Kanter, R. (1997). *On the frontiers of management.* Boston: Harvard Business School Press.

Katzenbach, J., & Smith, D. (1993, March–April). The discipline of teams. *Harvard Business Review, 71,* 111–120.

Knauer, K. (Ed.). (2009). Abraham Lincoln: An illustrated history of his life and times (a bicentennial celebration). *Time.*

Kouzes, J., & Posner, B. (1987). *The leadership challenge: How to keep getting extraordinary things done in organizations.* San Francisco: Jossey-Bass.

Kouzes, J., & Posner, B. (2002). *The leadership challenge* (3rd ed.). San Francisco: Jossey-Bass.

Lambert, L. (1998). *Building leadership capacity in schools.* Alexandria, VA: ASCD.

Little, J. W. (1982, May). Keynote address to Napa mentor teachers, Napa, CA.

Marzano, R., Waters, T., & McNulty, B. (2005). *School leadership that works.* Alexandria, VA: ASCD.

McGovern, G. (2009). *Abraham Lincoln.* New York: Henry Holt.

McKenzie, K., Christman, D., Hernandez, F., Fierro, E., Capper, C., Dantley, M., Gonzales, M., Cambron-McCabe, N., & Scheurich, J. (2008, February). From the field: A proposal for educating leaders for social justice. *Educational Administration Quarterly, 44*(1), 111–138.

McPherson, J. (1991). *Abraham Lincoln and the second American revolution.* New York: Oxford University Press.

McPherson, J. (2008a). *Tried by war.* New York: Penguin Press.

McPherson, J. (2008b). A. Lincoln, commander in chief. In E. Foner (Ed.), *Our Lincoln: New perspectives on Lincoln and his world* (pp. 19–36). New York: W. W. Norton.

McPherson, J. (2009, Winter). Commander in chief. *Lincoln: America's greatest president at two hundred* (*Smithsonian* collector's edition), 34–43.

Miller, W. (2002). *Lincoln's virtues: An ethical biography.* New York: Alfred A. Knopf.

Neeley, M. (2009). Lincoln and the Constitution. In S. Wilentz (Ed.), *The best American history essays on Lincoln* (pp. 229–243). New York: Palgrave Macmillan.

Newmann, F., & Wehlage, G. (1995). *Successful school restructuring.* Madison, WI: University of Wisconsin Press.

Oakes, J. (2007). *The radical and the republican: Frederick Douglass, Abraham Lincoln, and the triumph of antislavery politics.* New York: W. W. Norton.

Oakes, J. (2008). Natural rights, citizenship rights, states rights, and black rights. In E. Foner (Ed.), *Our Lincoln: New perspectives on Lincoln and his world* (pp. 109–134). New York: W. W. Norton.

Oates, S. (1977). *With malice toward none.* New York: Harper and Row.

Obama, B. (2006). *The audacity of hope.* New York: Crown.

Obama, B. (2009, Spring). What the people need done. *For the People* (A Newsletter of the Abraham Lincoln Association), *2*(1), 1–3. Speech delivered on February 12, 2009, in Springfield, IL, by President Barack Obama at the 200th anniversary celebration of the birth of President Lincoln, sponsored by the Abraham Lincoln Association.

Orfield, G., Losen, D., Wald, J., & Swanson, C. (2004). Losing our future: How minority youth are being left behind by the graduation rate crisis. Cambridge, MA: The Civil Rights Project at Harvard University. Available: www.urban.org/uploadedPDF/410936_LosingOurFuture.pdf

Palmer, P. (2008, Spring). On the edge. *Journal of Staff Development, 29*(2), 12–16.

Peterson, K. (1982). Making sense of principal's work. *Australian Administrator, 3*(3), 1–4.

Phillips, D. (1992). *Lincoln on leadership.* New York: Warner Books.

Reeves, D. (2006). *The learning leader.* Alexandria, VA: ASCD.

Reeves, D. (2009). *Leading change in your school.* Alexandria, VA: ASCD.

Robbins, P., & Alvy, H. (2004). *The new principal's fieldbook.* Alexandria, VA: ASCD.

Robbins, P., & Alvy, H. (2009). *The principal's companion* (3rd ed.). Thousand Oaks, CA: Corwin Press.

Sagor, R. (2009). Cultivating optimism in the classroom. In M. Scherer (Ed.), *Engaging the whole child* (pp. 45–54). Alexandria, VA: ASCD.

Schlechty, P. (2001). *Shaking up the schoolhouse: How to support and sustain educational innovation.* San Francisco: Jossey-Bass.

Senge, P. (1990). *The fifth discipline.* London: Century Business.

Sergiovanni, T. (2009). *The principalship* (6th ed.). Boston: Pearson.

Shenk, J. W. (2005). *Lincoln's melancholy.* Boston: Houghton Mifflin.

Sinha, M. (2008). Allies for emancipation? Lincoln and black abolitionists. In E. Foner (Ed.), *Our Lincoln: New perspectives on Lincoln and his world* (pp. 167–196). New York: W. W. Norton.

Smith, M. K. (2005). Bruce W. Tuckman—Forming, storming, norming and performing in groups. *The Encyclopaedia of Informal Education.* Retrieved October 2, 2009, from www.infed.org/thinkers/tuckman.htm

SooHoo, S. (1993). Students as partners in research and restructuring schools. *The Educational Forum, 57*(4), 386–393.

Striner, R. (2006). *Father Abraham: Lincoln's relentless struggle to end slavery.* New York: Oxford University Press.

Thomas, B. (1952). *Abraham Lincoln.* New York: Barnes and Noble with Alfred A. Knopf.

Thomas, E., & Wolffe, R. (2008, November). Obama's Lincoln. *Newsweek, 152*(21), 28–32.

Tschannen-Moran, M. (2004). *Trust matters.* San Francisco: Jossey-Bass.

Tuckman, B. (1965). Developmental sequence in small groups. *Psychological Bulletin, 63*(6), 384–399. Retrieved October 2, 2009, from http://dennislearningcenter.osu.edu/references/GROUP%20DEV%20/ARTICLE.doc

12Manage. Stages of team development (Tuckman). *The Executive Fast Track.* Retrieved October 14, 2009, from http://www.12manage.com/methods_tuckman_stages_team_development.html

Villegas, A., & Lucas, T. (2007, March). The culturally responsible teacher. *Educational Leadership, 54*(6), 28–33.

Von Frank, V. (2009, September). Superintendent stays on course with personal learning plan. *The Learning System, 5*(1), 1, 6.

Waters, T., Marzano, R., & McNulty, B. A. (2004, April). Leadership that sparks learning. *Educational Leadership, 61*(7), 48–51.

Watzlawick, P., Weakland, J., & Fisch, R. (1974). *Change: Principles of problem formulation and problem resolution.* New York: Norton.

Wayne, L., & Kaufman, L. (2001, September 16). Leadership, put to a new test. *New York Times,* Sec. 3, pp. 1, 4.

White, J. (1987). Eugene Lang: Dreammaker to the kids of Harlem. *AGB Reports, 29*(3), 10–17.

White, R. (2009). *A. Lincoln: A biography.* New York: Random House.

Whitman, W. (1892/1964). *Prose works 1892, Volume II.* (F. Stovall, Ed.). New York: New York University Press.

Whyte, D. (1994). *The heart aroused.* New York: Currency.

Wilentz, S. (2009, July). Who Lincoln was. *The New Republic, 240*(4,863), 24–47.

Wills, G. (1992). *Lincoln at Gettysburg: The words that remade America.* New York: Simon and Schuster.

Wilson, D. (2006). *Lincoln's sword.* New York: Alfred A. Knopf.

Winik, J. (2001). *April 1865.* New York: Harper Perennial.

Zenger, J., & Folkman, J. (2002). *The extraordinary leader.* New York: McGraw-Hill.

Index

The letter *f* following a page number denotes a figure.

About the Authors

 **Harvey Alvy** served as a practicing principal for 14 years, gaining both elementary and secondary administrative experience. His teaching career began as an inner-city elementary school teacher in New York City. Alvy later taught in middle and high schools in the United States and abroad. His experience in multicultural international schools is extensive and includes the American School in Kinshasa, Zaire; the American International School in Israel; the American Embassy School in New Delhi, India; and Singapore American School. Alvy is a founding member of the Principals' Training Center for International Schools. In 1991, the National Association of Elementary School Principals selected him as a National Distinguished Principal for American Overseas Schools. In 2004, Alvy received the Eastern Washington University CenturyTel Faculty Achievement Award for Teaching Excellence.

Alvy earned a doctorate in Educational Administration from the University of Montana focusing on the problems of new principals. He conducts workshops, both nationally and internationally, on the newcomer to the principalship, instructional leadership, ethical leadership, characteristics of great teachers, shaping collaborative school cultures, educational trends related to supervision, and the leadership of Abraham Lincoln. His publications include *The New Principal's Fieldbook: Strategies for Success* (Robbins & Alvy, 2004), *The Principal's Companion: Strategies for Making the Job Easier* (Robbins & Alvy, 2009), *If I Only Knew. . . : Success Strategies for Navigating the Principalship* (Alvy

& Robbins, 1998), and in Mandarin, *The Principal Management Handbook: The American Principal's Approach to Successful Administration* (Liu & Alvy, 2007)

Alvy holds the William C. Shreeve Endowed Professorship in Educational Administration at Eastern Washington University. He can be reached at 312 Williamson Hall, Department of Education, EWU, Cheney, WA 99004. Phone: (509) 359-6093. E-mail: halvy@ewu.edu. Web site: http://www.ewu.edu/x21525.xml.

 **Pam Robbins** is an independent consultant who works with school systems, state departments of education, universities, professional organizations, and corporate clients across the United States, Canada, Europe, Great Britain, South America, and Asia. Her professional background includes work as a special and regular education teacher, a high school basketball coach, Director of Staff Development, Special Projects and Research for the Napa County Office of Education, and Director of Training for the North Bay California School Leadership Academy. Robbins has designed and delivered training for leadership academies throughout the United States and internationally for the Department of Defense Education Equity Division. She has also presented at ASCD's Professional Development Institutes. Robbins's publications include *How to Plan and Implement a Peer Coaching Program* (1991), *Emotional Intelligence Professional Inquiry Kit* (Robbins & Scott, 1997), *The New Principal's Fieldbook: Strategies for Success* (Robbins & Alvy, 2004), *The Principal's Companion: Strategies for Making the Job Easier* (Robbins & Alvy, 2009), *If I Only Knew . . .: Success Strategies for Navigating the Principalship* (Alvy & Robbins, 1998), and *Thinking Inside the Block Schedule: Strategies for Teaching in Extended Periods of Time* (Robbins, Gregory, & Herndon, 2000).

Robbins earned her doctorate in educational administration from the University of California, Berkeley, where she focused on the development of professional learning communities. Robbins conducts workshops on the topics of leadership, supervision, school culture, professional learning communities, organizational change, brain research and implications for quality teaching, mentoring, peer coaching, and presentation skills.

She can be reached at 1251 Windsor Lane, Mt. Crawford, VA 22841. Phone: (540) 828-0107. Fax: (540) 828-2326. E-mail: probbins@shentel.net. Web: http://user.shentel.net/probbins.